£1.25

CW01636607

Alert In The West

Oberleutnant *Willi Heilmann, July 1944.*

Alert In The West

A Luftwaffe Pilot On The Western Front

By Willi Heilmann

WRENS PARK

Alert In The West was first published in 1955

This edition published in 2003 by Wren's Park Publishing,
an imprint of W. J. Williams and Son Ltd, and by
arrangement with Cerberus Publishing Ltd.

British Library Cataloguing in Publication Data.
A catalogue record for this book is available from the British Library.

ISBN 0 905778 90 1

PRINTED AND BOUND IN GREAT BRITAIN.

Contents

PREFACE

WHY DID I write this book?

As a justification of the German soldier? No. A subject that needs no justification, needs no words.

In 1945, assailed by a superior enemy, we trod the bitter path trodden by our defeated soldiers. We learned how to be silent when the values which have always been prized in the history of all peoples were held to be invalid for us and dragged in the mud. We have lost our freedom, sacrificed our possessions and our health. We have buried our comrades and through the long years and in difficult battles we have forfeited everything we fought for.

One thing we did not lose: our love of our German land.

And that is why I have written this book so that our country may know that we love it just as much as we did in happier times, that we, too, in its darkest hour, are glad to be its sons and that in the spirit in which we fought for it we are willing to help it overcome its distress.

Were I to claim for my book anything further it would be a desire to show the German soldier as he was, as he thought, spoke and behaved, and by doing this I think that it is the best possible testimony I can bring for a better understanding of our present-day attitude towards current events.

WILLI HEILMANN.

Chapter One

AT THE last moment I yanked the stick to the left and pulled it hard back towards me. My right leg was extended until it felt cramped on the rudder while below me in the vertical turn the menacing iron girders of the Eiffel Tower flashed past like a ghostly nightmare. I had got away with it once more. With a sigh of relief I straightened up my Fw 190, looking round anxiously for my comrades.

Not a sign of them!

This could easily happen in the murky twilight with the clouds at 300 feet in a raging thunderstorm.

For more than half an hour I had been circling over Paris with the last eight aircraft of my *Staffel*. Sheets of rain lashed against the cockpit. The windscreen wiper was unfortunately-covered with oil and once more I had to use the petrol flushing apparatus to clean the perspex. The squalls battered against the sides of the Focke and despite its 300 miles an hour it was tossed about like a cork.

There, just below on the left, was an airfield!

A sharp bank to reconnoitre the possibilities of landing. It was a good field. The landing mark and the usual sausage could not be seen. Well, that was not so bad; one always knew more or less the direction of the wind. Get ready for landing. Throttle back... lower the wheels...

Hell! What a witch's cauldron. Red and yellow tracers hissed past the cockpit from all sides. Those chaps obviously had not recognized my Focke or else... a quick look behind me.

No, there was no one on my tail. I dived sharply and flew low over the airfield. The nervous flak gunners had obviously not seen me waggle my wings. I must get out of here as quickly as possible. A thought suddenly struck me. There must be enemy aircraft over Paris. For half an hour I had been trying in vain to get into contact with some ground station. Their RT was not tuned in to operational lengths and I could not expect any help from the station in the Cologne-Osthtim sector.

The Sacré Cœur, the Moorish edifice on Montmartre, slipped past to starboard. The rain had ceased at last, but this was no weather for a low-altitude flight over Paris. With a trembling hand I wiped the sweat from my face and automatically switched on my navigation lights. Yes, that must be it. The flares... red.... red... red. I must land in ten minutes at the latest, for my fuel was almost exhausted. The red safety lamps had already been flickering for some moments on the instrument panel.

Another airfield – Le Bourget – the great airport of the capital. A crazy chaos of bomb craters and destroyed military and transport aircraft. No, Heilmann... You can't land a 2,000-hp fighter on a terrain like that. You're not a recce plane like the Fieseler Storch.

Two fighters bore down upon me. I was just about to grab the firing button when I recognised my friends. A waggle of the wings... stick close to me... They closed in almost wing tip to wing tip like timorous rabbits. Now they, too, switched on their navigation lights – green... red... white. With a grim smile I thought of my flying orders: twenty replacement machines with newly fledged pilots for III *Gruppe* of *Jagdgeschwader* 54. They'd pull a long face. It couldn't matter less. I must get down on the deck while I still had a chance. Pity I hadn't taken a good look at the position of the Paris airfields on the map before I started, but our departure had come as some-what of a surprise and the veteran *Staffelkapitän*, a sergeant-pilot who had only just recovered from his latest wound, had said with great cocksureness that afternoon: "Just stick close to me, boys, and I'll get you to Villacoublay."

Well, what now?

I still had about five minutes' gas left. The red lamps began to twinkle threateningly. The three machines made a wide circle round the outskirts of the city. Another airfield. Was it Orly? It had been blitzed to hell. To starboard the Eiffel Tower loomed up again in the grey twilight. If we kept this course we must come to Versailles and the airfield we were looking for, Villacoublay. Eyes peered eagerly through the murky dusk. Versailles!

My port neighbour broke away sharply and disappeared from view. I watched him leave with surprise. Tally-ho! The lights of an airfield had suddenly gone on. Could that be Villa? The runway looked a trifle small from this height. Red and white lights marked the flare path. A turn to the left... the run-in... it was high time. I sighed as I pulled back the throttle and my speed gradually decreased. Now I could not rev up again under any circumstances. It was lunacy now that the engine could conk out at any moment for lack of fuel. So there was nothing for it but to do the officially banned side-slip. Full right rudder, the joystick slightly to the left... give her a little more to bank more steeply. The Focke-Wulf fell like a heap of sacking.

Now what the hell was up? Red flares being fired ahead of me. The ground lights were quickly extinguished. God in heaven! A Focke was cruising in from the opposite direction to land. Had the fellow completely lost his nerve trying to land on this tiny strip down-wind? A second shadow appeared behind him. It was completely crazy! With compressed lips I pushed the throttle forward. A few air bumps... Careful not to stall. Then the screaming engine lifted the Focke just over the heads of the landing machine. Christ! Another one coming in from the wrong direction. They had all gone completely nuts.

Two of my own men were still on my tail. They were the same two who had tagged on and accompanied me for the last ten minutes. Now on no account must lack as if I had stage fright. No use thinking of what might happen if the fuel gave out. A new run-in. It was now almost dark. The lane of red and white lights and the red circle round the airfield showed up clearly. When my nose is pointing on that white line I must start to land again. Well, here goes, I thought. That'll do fine... Undercarriage lowered, landing flaps down, reduce gas and now slowly back with the stick. A slight side-slip... careful, keep her steady. Put her down... Automatically my hand manoeuvred the control column. A slight bump... Brakes on.

A swaying to left, and right. I was already at the edge of the field. Friendly lights twinkled up at the Focke. I had chosen the smallest airfield in the neighbourhood – Buc, a few miles south of Versailles.

A cigarette. A mechanic offered me a light. They all began to talk excitedly to me. They had watched my aircraft for a long time but they dared not give any recognition signal. There were American Thunderbolts about. The evening fighter-bomber patrol making a tour of the Paris airfields. Where were the others? An ambulance sped across the airfield with the crash wagon behind it. So someone had crashed. The three Fockes that had come in down-wind all lay wrecked at the edge of the field. The first one stood on its nose, so did the second... It was blazing. The third pilot looked away in horror, made the thumbs-down sign for a bad landing and wrote off his own undercarriage. Now the last machine was landing. Too fast... He was a novice. He came in well but, as was to be expected, the runway was too short. Another brand-new machine on its nose. Four hundred thousand marks had gone west!

"Manz," said the Doc, introducing himself. A slim, very elegant MO wearing a very smart uniform...

" I'm Heilmann."

My eyes glanced absentmindedly at the deep scars on the doctor's left cheek. Funny... only the gold ear-ring seemed to be missing. Then I noticed the row of medals, the Iron Cross First Class, won on active service... Ah, the Stalingrad Order. So there were still gentlemen who could de-ice themselves from the Eastern Front.

"Nice work, that," said the doctor gravely polishing his glasses with a handkerchief.

" Atishoo..."

"One of them has serious burns, a *Gefreiter*. The other, a *Feldwebel*, has swallowed some petrol, more petrol than is good for his stomach."

" Can you give me a lift? "

A Hansa drew up. The engine purred softly. I must get some sleep, I thought. What I need now is a decent bed...

"Are you operational?" asked the doctor at the steering wheel, interrupting my thoughts.

"No. We're from Fighter Group West. Reinforcements for III./JG 54."

"Hmm. You should have flown on a few miles." The doctor looked sharply at me. " We seldom get a visit here except from our friends on the other side. As you can imagine, they're not very popular. They pay us a visit every evening."

"Are we far now?"

"No, just on the corner there. I have my own-hospital almost next to my flat," said Dr Manz with a smile. "Have a cigarette?"

"Thanks." A match lit up our faces. I inhaled the smoke greedily into my lungs. The car turned to the right and the doctor pulled up outside a house.

"Here we are. Bring your gear along with you. You're my guest tonight." The doctor went on ahead. It seemed to be a typical Parisian residential quarter. A lot of reinforced concrete, glass, fresh air, comfortable rooms. I wrinkled my nose. A smell of carbolic... – "So you're a big medicine man, eh?" I asked good humouredly.

"You have to have them, you know."

A door opened to our right. Two hospital orderlies saluted.

"Are the wounded already here?"

"Yes, sir. We took the *Gefreiter* straight to Clichy. The *Feldwebel* is still unconscious."

"I'll take a look at him."

The elder of the two orderlies sprang to attention and opened the door, which led to the sick ward. A warm musty air greeted us as we entered. I stubbed out my cigarette.

"Well, Wimmers, how does he look?" said the doctor, turning to a small, rather puny soldier who was attending the casualty. He stood aside.

"I'm glad you've come, doctor," the man said anxiously without taking his eyes from the patient. "Seems to be worse than we thought. You can't move him without his groaning.

When the doctor turned the light full on the man lying in bed I opened my eyes wide. It was the sergeant-pilot responsible for leading in the *Staffel*. I remembered his reassuring, rather superior smile when he had said: "Just stick close to me, boys..." That was only three hours ago...

And now he was lying there with serious octane poisoning. The doctor examined the man calmly. Something seemed to be wrong with his left leg. He called for a splint. A contusion was clearly visible. "Could be a fracture," said the doctor. The wounded man groaned suddenly in his unconsciousness and retched... retched again. Numbly the poisoned body rebelled. The orderly quickly held out a shallow bowl; he was too late. The stinking mess soiled the blue check blanket. "That's good," said Dr Manz to me. "The more he can be sick the better it is. You can't be too careful with these bloody petrol poisonings and he's making my work easier. I may not have to use a stomach pump on him."

After Dr Manz had given his instructions, assuring the orderly that he would soon return, he took me aside and we left the room together.

"You needn't worry, my friend. We're always pleased when it goes off as harmlessly as that."

He led the way down a long passage. "Be careful, we mustn't show a light here. The whole corridor wall is practically one large glass window, like a studio. You'll see for yourself tomorrow morning." He opened a door, fumbled a little until he found the light switch. A comfortably furnished room lit by the warm light of a wall bracket met my eyes.

"Make yourself at home, Heilmann. I must get back to work. The door there leads to a small cubicle which will be your home until tomorrow morning. Go and have a lie down. I shan't be long." Before he reached the door he turned round again and pointed to a divan against the wall. "You'll find everything you want here. I know you pilots are a bit spoiled, but my cigars and the schnapps aren't too bad. You can make it up to me the next time I come over to Villa. In any case your *Gruppen Kommandeur* is a fine fellow. I'm merely telling you that to put your mind at rest."

"Why, to put my mind at rest?" I asked with a smile.

"Well, I suppose you're not expecting any bouquets for your forced landing. Oh, wait a minute. I've forgotten the most important thing." The sympathetic face grinned sardonicalIy from the door. "If you're taken short in the night you'll find the toilet in the corridor just outside the door. You can find it in the dark."

He switched off the light. I flung open the window. I could not bear this heavy cigar-laden atmosphere just before going to sleep. I remained spellbound at the window looking at the enchanting picture outside The bright light of the moon bathed the capital in a silver veil. So the house stood on high ground. Pity, I'd forgotten to ask in what quarter of the outskirts of Paris I now was.

No sound disturbed the warm July night.

So here I am once more in Paris, I thought. It was three years since I, who had just got my commission, had been posted from Arras to the God-forsaken hole Raczky, near Suwalki, in Poland... A few miles away through the forest on the far side of the river lay Augustow. That had been their marching direction and it could only be days before they launched a decisive attack. At that time the problem of Soviet Russia had lain like a nightmare over the troops. The presentiment, the fear that had lain like a leaden weight on the heart, that terrifying vital question – How far would the German army still have to march before it could defeat the enemy – had proved to be well founded...

Now the new and the final decision of this murderous war stood before them. For eight days now in Normandy there had been a bitter struggle for each foot of soil. Should the invasion succeed – and it had actually succeeded – then this twentieth-century Seven Years War was drawing to a close.

The wail of sirens interrupted the flow of my thoughts. In a flash searchlights raked the sky in a confused network exploring, feeling for enemy aircraft. Harsh contours of torn clouds were lit up in a ghostly light. Barking flak, explosions, the usual routine...

Below in the street hasty footsteps, anxious cries, oaths... Men in distress. Here in Paris as on the Rhine where I had spent two days of my last leave... Men pursued by bombs, desperate, bewildered and out of their minds. How much longer must they continue in this misery?

"We must not weaken," I murmured to myself. "There's no room for sentimentality among fighter pilots." I lay down. Ah, a pillow! After four years of army camp-beds it reminded me strangely of leave. If only my head would stop buzzing – the after-effects of that nerve-racking night landing. I could not get out of my head a sentimental melody; it had come to my mind when I was standing by the window, that soft alien tune which had so little to do with war and grief, *Sous les toits de Paris...*

Chapter Two

I PUSHED the throttle slowly forward. The Focke shuddered under the power of full engine. I was pressed back in my seat from the force of acceleration. Keeping the aircraft's nose straight with the rudder, I roared over the smooth concrete of the runway. 60... 80... 90... 100... showed on the cockpit indicator. At 105 mph the Focke was airborne. Undercarriage knobs pressed and a slight drop in height showed that the wheels were up. A glance at the instrument-panel lamps... Port, green... starboard, green. Everything in order. Now the button for closing the flaps at the trailing edge of the wings, which had given additional lift to the aircraft on take-off. Throttle slightly back and another glance at the rev counter. The needle fell back to 3,450 rpm.

A left-hand turn and a last look over the wings at the airfield. It was far too small for a fighter. Leaving the Eiffel Tower on my left, I circled Paris once more. Old acquaintances came into view the Arc de Triomphe, the Madeleine, and that must be the dome of the Invalides and the Louvre away to the left.

A gentle left-hand turn and the heights of Montmartre appeared in the bright morning light. Then the Sacré Cœur, a white alien beauty in the heart of the West. Nothing had been destroyed. Obviously the Ville Lumière was being spared. The environs, on the other hand, looked desolate... No station, no bridge and no main road without the grim traces of bombing.

That must be the Bois de Boulogne below my right wing, with St Germain beyond and the castle slightly to one side. In the spring of 1940 my pioneer company had been transferred there from Rouen to take part in the great victory parade in the Champs Elysées. It was eventually cancelled but I had never forgotten those magnificent hours of rest and relaxation.

A turn to the right and a burst of speed. Now I could see the beautiful artificial lake surrounded by terraced orchards of peach trees. The familiar tennis court gleamed like a red eye and the white villa was still there. Yes, that was the land of enchantment, the land of happy memory.

I smiled when I thought of my former mates. Cunning old Brehmer, fat Brendel, the good-natured draughtsman from Frankfurt with the black rascally eyes, and Williax from Kassel... Where had they all got to now?

Down there on the lake in the shade of the fruit trees they had once skylarked with a girl. An exuberant chase had begun with much splashing of water. Yvonne had paddled helplessly round in circles and the three of them had teased her like lascivious fauns until she took to flight; the Three Musketeers failed to find her because she was hiding coyly in the bushes.

Snap out of it. You mustn't start dreaming, Heilmann. Hedge-hopping's forbidden in the neighbourhood of Paris unless you want to get a powerful "rocket". Nor is the gleaming blue sky a healthy spot for a fighter. Enemy spotters might be about. Split-arse turns... I flew over Colombes along the Seine, turning southwards from Montmartre to the Eiffel Tower; it looked decidedly more attractive in daylight. I preferred it that way. The memory was still fresh of the spectre with its fatal network of iron girders that had loomed out of the darkness during the storm of the previous evening... Right-hand turn... Versailles. And behind it that wretched little airfield, Buc... and then Villacoublay.

My own home, if one could call it that.

But hell! Where shall I land, I suddenly thought. No indication... This airfield is in use but so is that one on the other side of the road. No one mentioned the fact that Villa had two airfields!

My decision was made quickly on military reasoning. Well, north and south. Which is our dump? It's obviously a toss-up. The north looks far better, so that seems to imply that the south must be the fighters' eyrie...

I was right. At the side of the flarepath I spotted the camouflaged fighters in their dispersal pens. Mechanics rushed up. I raised my canopy.

"Is III./JG 54 stationed here?"

"No, you've come to the wrong shop," drawled one of the ground staff with a Berlin accent.

"But there are fighters over there." I did not need to wait for an answer. They were fighters all right, but they had pointed noses and small bandy legs. They were the famous and much-hated Messerschmitt 109s.

"Just my luck," I grumbled. "It seems I'm doomed not to find the 'Green Hearts'."

"Ah, so that's where you want to go? This place is driving me nuts, but don't worry, *Herr Oberleutnant*" – he cast a look at the two stripes on my flying suit – "you won't have to take off again. It often happens," and he pointed with two red flags to the left of the field. "The Frenchies are quite used to it."

And while I, still at a loss, looked in the direction in which the man was pointing, a wide gate opened, two long poles fell and barred the busy main road... The traffic waited and I taxied the Focke slowly on to the other airfield. I had reached Villacoublay North. I had envisaged an impressive landing with nineteen other Fockes but now I arrived on my own, like a lost bird too tired to fly, slowly creeping into its new nest.

A fine start, Heilmann! What will your new CO, your future flying mates and all those who witness your arrival think of this resurrected Don Quixote?

The Focke was now in its pen and the mechanic had already thrown green camouflage nets over the "crate". A pair of questioning eyes met mine. "Where shall I take your gear, *Herr Oberleutnant*?"

"Oh, leave it all here for the moment. I don't know where I'm going myself."

The *Oberfeldwebel* stopped a passing motorbike and sidecar. "Take the *Leutnant* over there, half right among the tall trees. That's headquarters."

This is a pretty large airfield, I thought. You can't do much about it on foot. The motor-cyclist stopped. "Thanks, I don't need you any more." Flying suit straightened, the angle of the cap adJusted, belt fastened... the hundred-times-practised routine details. I was still carrying my flying helmet with the earphones.

I came to a swing door; someone muttered: "Excuse me, *Herr Oberleutnant*" and I was inside. On my left a *Gefreiter* – he turned out later to be the orderly-room clerk – was following a confused babble and wild cries in his radio. Bending forward, his mouth open and his ear to the loudspeaker, stood an officer. This atmosphere of easy-come easy-go, of unshaven faces and men in shirt-sleeves immediately impressed me. I was in the front line now even though outside I caught a glimpse through an open door of a table laid with coffee cups and two men playing ping-pong. I had seen the same thing, of course, in Russia when as adjutant of the Army General Staff I had visited *Oberst* Trautloft and his fighters at Siwerskaya.

"Rabe Anton[1] calling. Tally-ho!"

The two men at the loudspeaker suddenly sprang to life. "Kurt... he's got his fourth," called the man in shirt-sleeves to the two tennis players and clapped his hands with delight. As he turned round he saw me.

He gave me a quick look.

"I'm Neumann," and, realising that he was in a polo shirt, added: "*Hauptmann* Neumann, the Adjutant."

"Heilmann, sir, from Fighter Group West posted to III./JG 54 as from June the 12th."

A handshake, rather limp and damp, the sort of handshake I did not very much like.

"You can hear them now. They're near Caen, a bit to the east. Four shot down so far..."

"Rabe Anton to all aircraft... Garden hedge[2]."

"It's all over. Let's hope things have gone well," said the Adjutant, making his way towards the office.

"Come with me, please. What did you say your name was ?"

"Heilmann, *Herr Hauptmann*."

Pushing the door open with his left foot, a small stocky *Gefreiter* in a

[1] Code name for the *Gruppen Kommandeur.*
[2] Code word for "Return to base".

white drill jacket balanced a dozen plates of food and looked for a place to put them down. He elbowed aside a few wooden models of aircraft on the table and set his burden down on the empty space.

"The greater the commotion the more the shepherd worries about his flock," and, switching off the radio, he went on grumbling. "The old man's a bit jittery. Good thing we've got some decent grub today."

"Well, Kaluweit, what have you got for us today"

"Ah, sit over there in the corner, *Herr Oberfähnrich*.[3] There's a lovely roast with sauerkraut."

"Hmm!" came a grunt of pleasure from the corner. A small table and four upholstered chairs, a bookshelf, a few dog-eared newspapers and magazines, packs of cards, chess, and draughts all in a jumble as though they had just been used... Behind a French magazine sat a lanky fellow in shirt-sleeves and shorts with a pipe stuck in the corner of his mouth.

And then there was a great din outside the door, a jostling and shedding of flying suits such as always happens when the first pilots return from ops to their stations.

The pilot officer hastily grabbed a stick which looked more like a clumsy truncheon and lumbered up from his corner. I could see that his right leg was in plaster. His broad, bony fingers pushed the long red hair back from his forehead.

Kaluweit kicked open the door. "Well, boys, how did it go?" His red-cheeked East Prussian face beamed at the newcomers. "Two... three... five... seven – ah, we're all here," he said cheerfully.

"No, Fritzie, the Chief's not back. I saw one go down with a black trail of smoke. Let's hope he got out of it."

"He's a crazy bastard," said a very pale young NCO pilot. It wouldn't be a bad thing for us if he was put on ice for a bit."

" Don't talk like that..."

"Teumer is a fine bloke, doesn't know what fear is..."

"I know, but we're the ones to cop it. He's always the first to wade in and then they tickle us up behind him."

In the meantime Kaluweit had laid the table. A few cigarettes were lit and peace was gradually restored.

The tall pilot officer took a *Feldwebel* aside.

"Well, Kurt, how did it go?"

"Same as usual. We can't get to the mouth of the Orne as we used to. They are beginning to attack us at Evreux now, and at the latest by Lisieux. We seem to have been lucky this time except for Teumer. You can congratulate me – I got a Lightning."

"Fine, Kurt... Good luck!"

"Yes, *Feldwebel*, I saw it. Make your report and I'll sign below it as witness," called a pale NCO pilot from the other side of the table.

"Thanks, Hunger. Thanks..."

"So our Venjakob has got his dozen," said lanky Ostro – his features and accent betrayed that he was an East Pomeranian. The boys called him Patt.

[3] No British or American equivelant but this rank was that of an 'officer candidate' – in this case a 'Senior Officer Candidate' and would be of 'Warrant Officer' level.

"If Teumer doesn't get back he'll lead the *Staffel*. There's a shortage of officers here right up to staff rank."

"That would be dandy," said Hunger. He had not been long with the *Staffel* and the nerve-racking dog-fights over the bridgehead were obviously getting him down. Also he didn't seem particularly fond of *Leutnant* Teumer his *Staffelkapitän*. It was not much fun sticking close to such a skilful madcap as Teumer.

"Come on, youngsters, grub's getting cold," grumbled Fritz Kaluweit. They could in fact have been his youngsters, for he carried forty to forty-five years on his broad back and somewhere in the neighbourhood of Goldaper his family waited for him – his mother and little Eva.

"*Mahlzeit*, boys!"

The CO broke up the party. "Come along with me, please, Heilmann, and you too, Gross and Dortenmann. Do you want to come, Emil, or..."

"You said it, Robert." The man called Emil laughed gaily.

"Well, give my love to the girl friend." And then, turning to me, "He's got a nice little piece in the canteen at Versailles. Our 'Bully'!"

I went off with this cheerful group of officers to the next room, where, beneath a green carved wooden heart escutcheon, we found a number of comfortable leather armchairs. An orderly quickly brought in the pilots' favourite after-dinner drink, cups of fragrant coffee, with cakes and Turkish cigarettes. I began to feel at home among my new comrades.

So this was Robert Weiss – "a fine fellow" Dr Manz had called him yesterday – *Kommandeur* of III *Gruppe* in the famous '*Grünherz*' *Geschwader* which held the record for enemies shot down on the invasion front. My eyes wandered from the Knight's Cross to his eyes. I considered myself to be a good judge of men, and this boy's eyes seemed to be the right sort – frank, open, although they were a slightly watery blue. He was the oldest in this circle apart from the non-flying staff officers. On the other side of the table, almost swallowed up in an armchair, sat *Leutnant* Alfred Gross. He had been promoted officer for bravery. Next to him was *Leutnant* Dortenmann... slightly cold and reserved.

" Heilmann," said *Hauptmann* Weiss, interrupting my thoughts, "you'll take over *Leutnant* Teumer's *Staffel* 7."

Turning to the others he went on, "Maybe he's got away with it again."

"Ah, a Viennese," I said to myself, as I heard the soft accent.

"He could still have jumped but he seems to have been caught by the tail unit. Legs broken." And then to me "In the air, *Feldwebel* Venjakob will take over the *Staffel*. You'll stick to me. I want to see what you can do."

"What's happened to the new 'crates' that have been announced?" he called over to another table where a game of skat was in progress.

"Well, that's quite a long story and a painful one," replied Neumann.

I grew uneasy. Had the time come for me to speak up...?

"Nine out of the twenty have reported, including *Herr* Heilmann," said Neumann, laying down his cards. "Eight landed here during the fighter-bomber attack last night. *Herr* Heilmann arrived only an hour ago."

"I forced-landed at Buc last night, sir," I said, clearing my throat.

"But why?" asked the *Gruppen Kommandeur* with surprise.

I gave my report. The two *Leutnants* could not disguise a quiet grin when a surly "Idiot" came from the lips of Weiss.

"Yes, sir," I said, looking him straight in the face.

"Oh, not you: I mean *Gruppen Kommandeur* Steinert. Fancy expecting an operational officer with silver wings to find his own airfield. Typical just at the time I need pilots so urgently.

"I'm not surprised they get jittery when they go into action for the first time. Those half-wits at home won't do a stroke more than necessary. All they care about is getting things ready – so many here, and so many there. How they arrive is of no possible interest to the worthy 'kiwis' from Cologne-Ostheim Command. Get the 'crates' away quiclcly from the airfield: whether or not they're ready for ops is quite another matter."

The mood at the skat table began to grow heated. A slam hand was laid on the table card by card, making the glasses rattle.

The telephone rang. The orderly took off the receiver and called the *Gruppen Kommandeur.*

"Hold on a minute, please. Neumann, take it down..."

" Yes, sir." Neumann with the second receiver to his ear wrote down on his skat block: *Free fight in the Evreux-Elbeaf sector. Fighter-bombers.* This was the new mission.

Chapter Three

The invasion front, 20th July 1944

"STICK it out, stick it out," is the order of the day. The battle has become so tough that there is no tomorrow, only today and the decision of the moment.

My first dog-fights are now behind me. Wherever we appear we find an oppressive enemy superiority. My poor country looking in vain for German fighters in the sky, if only you had some idea how uncomplainingly your pilots go to their death as they carry out their orders! For eight days now I have been leading *Staffel* 7. During this time we have lost 50 per cent of our aircraft and every fifth pilot is a casualty... burns, broken limbs, dead...

I closed my diary. I felt tired and there were dark circles under my eyes. My veins stood out on the back of my hands betraying the tension and strain on the heart and the nervous system.

When a few minutes previously the news had come through of an attempt on the life of the Führer, the men showed little emotion. I said what I had to say as an officer bound by my military oath. At the same time I knew, as every other fighter pilot here knew, that I must go on fighting and flying for my country even though there was no possibility of winning the war.

The hopelessness of the situation turned many of those who went on fighting into mercenaries. They must not be judged. There were no cowards in the ranks of the fighter arm.

But no one can judge what it meant to be airborne in a few minutes, a futile and hopeless mission against overwhelming odds; a short dog-fight and then a rapid scramble for home because the enemy came in from every quarter to the help of their friends and neither the finest flying technique nor the craziest bravery was of any avail. You had to disappear from the scene of your fight... You simply had to get away whether you wanted to or not. To remain in the battle was suicide.

And to complete the cup of bitterness, those impossible flying orders. The mistrust of the ground staff who dictated the path of death from safe cellars or from comfortable dug-outs far to the rear of Paris. Ignorance, often malice and treacherous sabotage, insisted that good communication and the natural desire to make things difficult or even impossible for the enemy demanded a certain altitude; as a result of this a *Staffel* was "led" for hundreds of miles at 600 feet while enemy *Staffeln* as numerous as the stars in the sky and cruising at all altitudes dived like vultures on the *Staffeln* of the Damned.

There was no mutiny! Loyalty held the *Staffeln* together and the Commanding Officer had to sort it out for himself how he detailed his men. Desertion to the enemy never occurred despite all his blandishments. German upbringing and character forbade it.

Flung into this madness of the last years of the war, no man found the way of salvation. They obeyed their orders and were pursued by the Devil.

⋆ ⋆ ⋆

The *Gruppe* flew peacefully on a north-easterly course.

The "*Grünherz*" in the van: the *Gruppen Kommandeur* with his flight. I flew behind him in command of *Staffel* 7. Above me to starboard Dortenmann, and to port, somewhat to the rear, Fred Gross with twelve aircraft. Six hundred feet higher *Hauptmann* Lang with *Staffel* 9 – "Bully" still preferred the job of "spotter". In the second and third wave followed other flights of Fw 190s. High above us in the morning sunlight gleamed the tiny bodies of the Me 109s – the new type with increased performance designed as altitude fighters. All in all, there were about 150 fighters, so apparently the whole armada had been sent to the invasion area.

"Rabe Anton" led. This time at a great height – between twelve thousand and eighteen thousand feet – with thousand pound bombs hanging beneath the bodies. These were destined for the concentration of shipping at the mouth of the Orne.

Radio silence had been ordered... No conversation between the individual aircraft. Over the intercom "Prima donna", the ground-direction radio station on the Eiffel Tower, had given its last directions and air reports to "Rabe Anton". To the north appeared the familiar, much-feared sector... the Channel.

Flying to port astern of the *Gruppen Kommandeur*, I could feel the nervous tension reigning among the whole formation. Ice-cold, my heart beat resolutely and my eyes sought the target. There it was. Below us to port, gleaming leaden-white, was the baggy crater of the Orne estuary. The English fleet lay like slim black pencils tied up in big bundles. Thick fat lumps among them – the transports which were to be bombed...

The aircraft turned sharply north-eastwards in order to attack out of the sun, its bright rays behind them making things difficult for the defence when they dived. Commands from Rabe Anton... "Choose your targets... Sight-screens on..." The white circles with the cross-wires on the glass screen lit up clearly. The electric firing apparatus was set and the firing buttons ready for firing...

The Fockes dived on their target from 12,000 feet. 400... 450... 500 mph. The aircraft shuddered and vibrated, screaming as a result of the high demands made upon it. The wings left behind long milky vapour trails in the blue morning sky. The ack-ack guns began to blaze away. The tracers hissed past the cockpits in a diabolical yellow-red rain of fire. Huge banks of cloud were formed by the black woolly balls of smoke from the shell-bursts. I hunched my head in my shoulders. At this high speed my blood coursed fast and my eyes stood out on stalks. The lids began to burn. My mouth was wide open...

Bomb tit pressed... on the release above the target a thick black box appeared in the sights. Desperate defence fire from all the rapid-firing guns pursued the aircraft, the ack-ack from the ships being the most accurate.

And now the worst: to get out of this witch's cauldron into which from all sides "Indians" now streaked to protect the ships. Normally after a low-level attack it was the easiest thing in the world to get away, but in this case it was impossible, for the region was far too well protected. In the neighbourhood of Caen stood a close-set hedge of barrage balloons and the wires would have cut off our wings. No fighter would choose to wage a dog-fight in a balloon barrage.

The only thing to do was to regain height. I stuck close to the *Kommandeur*, my engine flat out. Over the RT came the first indications of a developing air battle. The desperate cries of men in great danger broken by calm voices of the individual *Staffelkapitaen*. An occasional "Tally-ho" announcing a bitter struggle and a victory. When a clear voice screamed: "Spitfire, Spitfire. I can't shake him off. Help me," I shut off my radio. I told myself that the most experienced pilots would be feeling scared and prefer to shut off their radios. The *Kommandeur* had reached a bank of clouds. Directly below us Bully was rallying his flock and I could easily see their yellow numbers. The "*Grünherz*" seemed to have come through well. Astern in a tornado of anti-aircraft fire I could see the wild circus of "Indians" and "Bandits" circling each other like flights of hornets looking for a gap into which they could break to shoot each other down. Machines diving , to the ground, bursting into flames... Far behind, black smoke in columns from damaged ships, the glaring light of flickering flames... The horror of it...

I pulled the stick back into my stomach. Something black streaked just below my Focke. It was damned uncomfortablp in this cloud-bank. Was it a "Black Widow", the new black twin-fuselaged brother of the Lightning? Pity. Had I recognised it a fraction of a second earlier, I could have shot it down. The enemy must have had a fright too and be thinking the same thing.

And now I was with the *Staffel* again. About fifty Fockes had collected. Half-roll... I dived towards the Seine, the natural line, like a mother directing her wandering children.

* * *

Three hours later...

Scramble! Free-for-all attack between Alençon and Chartres on an approaching armada of Lightnings and Mustangs carrying out a low-level strafe of communication lines. *Leutnant* Dortenmann to lead. I took over a *Staffel* of sixteen Fockes. We climbed in steep spirals, for the advantage of height was half the battle in such an attack. Course 270°. We soon reached the hilly country west of Chartres. "Careful," Dortenmann was already calling over the RT, reporting "Indians" astern to port and somewhat below us. A moment later he broke off and I attacked from out of the sun. Not very favourable, I thought. In spite of reduced throttle he would still be travelling too fast and his approach was too steep.

My thoughts were interrupted... an automatic yanking of the machine and a change-over into steep turns. I could see the vapour trails forming behind my tail. You had to be very careful of Lightnings, for they had four cannon in the cockpit with the devastating effect of fire hoses.

"Heilmann to Dortenmann. Attacking from above you."

"Victor. Try and form defence circle."

Soon six Fockes were in a compact self-protecting circle; into which the attacking Mustangs could not break unless they were willing to run the danger of coming into the enemy's sights. While Dortenmann with the remaining ten machines was getting into position to attack from a superior altitude the Lightnings, which had been summoned to the aid of the Mustangs, came from below in sweeping climbing turns. There must have been thirty of them.

I could not be certain of anything, for three Mustangs lined up for the attack. A quick glance behind me. God be praised, White 4 – tall Patt's machine – was there. The merry-go-round began. Tracers... Missed him... Now from the starboard. Zoom. A kind of stall turn... Flatten out... Ah, a sitting bird. I was well on the tail of a Mustang. The American had sensed the danger and was throwing his trim Mustang all over the sky. Pity; my tracers did not get him and trailed off behind his tail. Tighter and tighter... The winner l would be the one who made the tightest turns. The sky below... then the wooded hills to starboard like a giant rock face swinging up to meet me. A strange world, but this was no time; for observations. It was a life-and-death struggle. The one who could fire first had a chance of survival and in this tough banking contest I forced the Mustang ever closer into my sights.

Another burst... In desperation the American tried to break away. Too late. He flew into the field of fire of my four heavy machine-guns and spun down towards the "deck" in flames.

I hardly had time to utter a hoarse "Tally-ho" from my dry throat. A Lightning irresponsibly showed its bright silver twin fuselage just below me. Quickly I turned the Focke over on its back. I yanked the stick so hard in my excitement that my head banged against the roof of the cockpit. A short burst... Unlucky. The Lightning had spotted its new foe and the wild chase was on again...

"Garden hedge" came over the RT "Dortenmann calling. Garden hedge. There are too many of them. Hedge-hop for home."

The manoeuvre did not come off. We were continually involved in bitter dog-fights with superior numbers of Americans who clung to the tails of the sixteen. Dortenmann pulled his red machine up into the air – Red 1. What had happened? It was pouring smoke.

"Bale out, Dortenmann. You're on fire," came a voice over the intercom.

White 10 roared past with two Lightnings on its tail. That was *Leutnant* Kurt Knebe who had flown a hundred missions but had not yet won the Iron Cross First Class. A nervous bird of ill omen who always got out of the craziest dog-fights.

"Look out, Heilmann." That was lanky Patt at my side. He flung his machine to one side. I followed suit.

Two Lightnings were pursuing a Focke. They were in a good position for Ostro and me. A burst, then a second, and while Patt announced his victory White 1 in front of me, was trying to shake off his enemy with desperate rolls and split-arse turns. Another well-aimed burst. The Lightning turned over on its back and went into a flat spin. Like a withered leaf it fluttered on fire in wide spirals to the ground. The pilot must have been wounded or perhaps killed, for no parachute opened.

I could not see the crash, for a whole mob dived on me from starboard. Two... four... five, I counted. Steep right-hand bank, dive... The engine was in difficulties and was not giving her full revs. Now I was alone. The Lightnings stuck grimly to my tail.

A vertical dive almost to the ground. Speed close on 600 mph. Vapour trails left and right above the wings... then nearer to the ground. I wonder what that comic clanking and ringing is, I thought in terror. The right wing had been hit. It had a number of holes through the centre section but the worst part was over.

Hedge-hopping, White 1 streaked over the trees. Instinctively I went below a high-tension cable and then eastwards. A glance over my shoulder. Three Lightnings were still in pursuit, but although they were too far away to fire they did not give up the chase. The Focke roared over the banks of the Seine. A tight right turn. The damaged wing tip nearly touched the ground. Straighten up. A farm flashed past. Then I reached the high embankment of the Seine... The Focke almost grazed the water. Here I had to pay great attention. Left, then right... In this narrow river valley with thirty-feet-high banks it was a matter of life and death. However, it was my only chance to shake off these obstinate Yanks. They were still there but they did not dare to come right down into the gully and try to cut me off, to get within range.

A bridge. The three broad stone piles caught my eye. Without time to reflect I had cold-bloodedly taken the Focke under the right span. A steep cliff loomed up before me dangerously near, but I knew now where I was. Soon the Eiffel Tower would be visible and behind this embankment the Oise must be flowing to the left. That would be my salvation...

Now I was almost safe. A sharp turn to the left as low as possible over the water, then a hop to the right over a small wood.

Looking over my shoulder I now saw that I was alone at last. My trick had succeeded. The Lightnings were still in the Seine valley.

St Denis appeared in the distance and, leaving Paris to starboard, I made a wide sweep southwards back to the airfield. Radio contact with my station was out of the question. I was flying too low. It did not matter. Things had gone well so far and I was sure that I would find the airfield clear. I soon reached Villacoublay. Two aircraft were taxying at speed to *Staffel* 7's dispersal pens which were hidden in a wood. A bank to the left, throttle down, a short zoom... undercarriage locked down.

The mechanics knew from the pilots who had already landed what had happened and were therefore not surprised that the new *Staffelkapitän* was soaked with sweat when he climbed out of the cockpit.

⋆ ⋆ ⋆

A moment later White 7 landed. The cockpit was missing and half the front windscreen had been shot away. This had happened to fair-haired Sergeant Pilot von der Jechten for the second time within a fortnight. He waved cheerfully to me as I rode in the motor-bike and sidecar on the way to headquarters to make my report. There the mood was high. The *Gruppe* had twelve victories to its credit with only two pilots lost. Dortenmann had baled out near Randonnai. The *Gruppen Kommandeur* was talking to him now on the telephone.

I made my report and was congratulated.

"Ah, so our fledgling is becoming independent," said Weiss, replacing the receiver and turning to me. "Well, carry on the good work."

Dortenmann remained absent for a few days. He had dropped near the Trappist monastery. He had been high enough to bale out but he had sprained his left ankle. He would soon be fit again for flying. For a bag of six Lightnings and five Mustangs, two Fockes fell flaming to the ground. There were no survivors.

"They must be *Leutnant* Marker and *Gefreiter* Hunger from your *Staffel*, Heilmann. They are the only ones who are still missing," broke in the Adjutant.

The orderly-room clerk brought me a schnapps.

"Umm. That does you good although it's so hot. Give me another one, please."

I sat down and told my story. The *Gruppen Kommandeur* astride one of the armchairs listened to my report of the engagement.

The pilots called the cosy break after meals the "nattering session". The Viennese CO had once called it this and the expression had stuck.

It was a cosy and comfortable messroom, a good place to relax. Pilots appreciate it like that. The officers' mess and the quarters of the flying NCOs were carefully and lovingly transformed into a pleasant home in the shortest possible time and the other services envied the Luftwaffe on account of this. The foot-slogger looked up from his world of filth and vermin enviously at the "cushy" life of the pilots and voiced his opinion about it in no uncertain fashion.

Were they right? I had been in the war from the very first day and received my first serious wound after the fourteen-day Polish campaign. My left leg was still a trifle numb and difficult to move. I, too, had cursed the "collar and tie" soldiers when, after living for weeks on end in the mud of the front line, I had gone to the rear and caught a glimpse of this feudal, privileged pilots' existence.

Now I could make my own comparisons. To my surprise I realised that this gentleman's life could be far worse than a week in the trenches.

On the one hand the infantryman is in his trench. He is occasionally packed off on leave or taken to rest behind the lines...

For him the front line is a farewell to life, and Dante's words – *Abandon hope all ye who enter here* – seem to hang over his head in the sinister fog of an uncertain future. Days and weeks passed demanding great self-sacrifices, days of fatigue and battles... days when the clock hand of the lucky ones turned too fast and they would have liked to halt its mad speed, others when deadly boredom piled up minutes to hours, days and weeks that added up to a torturing eternity.

And so, as beards grow and become painful on dirt-stained faces, linen begins to stink and itch, and their whole bodies are covered with lice – in short the soldier has become no better than a pig – the nerves become dulled and a state of imbecility makes it easier for human beings to endure their fate in cold blood. The reactions between feeling and intelligence are dead, and the blood flows turgidly between the heart and the brain.

Man has become the mere tool of Juggernaut, the war machine.

And then there is the pilot, the fighter-pilot flung at the speed of lightning into new situations, feverish and trembling like a thoroughbred horse at the gate. Each murderish contrast between a comfortable life and the stark antechamber of death plays on his emotions. On landing from ops he goes to his comfortable quarters; the coffee is still warm in the cups that have not yet been cleared away, but that cup... . and that one there... the orderly can clear them away, for the pilots who drank from them have been shot down by the enemy...

"Don't look so damned serious, old boy," laughed Gross.

"That's the lot for today, I think."

"Then we can stretch our legs for a bit."

"Who's going to make a third?" called Neumann. This old skat enthusiast, who often found the night too short for his eternal gambling, was looking for someone to complete the game.

Over in the corner, under a lamp made from a broken propeller bound with raffia sat Dortenmann and *Leutnant* Kersten, who had been three days with the "*Grünherz*". They were playing chess. Everyone was there, even Bully Lang. Weiss had put on his best uniform and was waiting for his car.

"Well, gentlemen, have you anything on? If not we could go and have some fun at the canteen. Let's say about five o'clock, eh?"

"Good idea, Robert. It's a long time since we've graced my girlfriend's round table. Let's have a real night out." Neumann had interrupted his game of skat and was advising the others to accept the *Kommandeur*'s invitation.

Everyone, in fact, was only too glad to accept. We all arranged to meet at the canteen in Versailles at five o'clock.

* * *

Things always turn out differently... I was barely dressed when the telephone rang. Kiks the orderly room clerk answered it. He broadcast the whole station but no one was to be found.

"Well, you've got one silly sheep to answer your bloody silly call. Where's the fire?".

"We've just got a late order for a scramble."

"Oh, hell. Where?"

"Dog-fight between Versailles and St Germain. There are Thunderbolts in the air."

"When do we go?"

"At once. The *Oberfeldwebel* has already reported which machines are airworthy."

"All right, spoil-sport. Take off in five minutes... at least a dozen aircraft."

I quickly put on my flying suit over my best uniform. *Hauptmann* Lang in a similar situation once flew at six o'clock in the morning in his pyjamas and had to bale out in them. Well, now my belt, the compass and my revolver. In a rage I slammed the door behind me as I went out...

What is there to tell of the engagement? It was the same as usual in such circumstances. The Thunderbolts were far too busy with their low-level attack on the road between St Germain and Evreux to spot the German fighters in time. ' The fourteen Fockes broke them up and the intruders had to run for their lives. One-nil in favour of the "*Grünherz*", but I remained in the fight too long and suddenly enemy help arrived. Now came the thick end of the stick...

My White 1 caught fire and I had to bale out. For the fifth time within three weeks I was hanging on my parachute. At barely 6,000 feet I was swaying over a small town. It was an unpleasant sensation. Hot and cold shivers ran up and down my spine. To jump in open country was child's play compared with this. Those roofs... the "brolly" could get caught up on a chimney, then I would be bumped about up there and have to wait for the firemen with their long ladders to rescue me. That was all right, but one could also be bashed against a roof and in such cases the parachute "torched" and all your bones were broken if you fell from thirty feet on to the pavement.

The people below had noticed the white parachute. Men began to run about gesticulating and staring up at it. A light breeze blew me the length of a broad street; I remained right in the middle between the houses. A bit of luck! Soon the earth grew closer and I saw a round, open space. During the last three hundred feet the houses seemed to rush up to meet me. I landed with a bump and was dragged along by the parachute, but hands were there ready to help me out of my harness. I opened my eyes in amazement. I must have looked like a moon calf. As though I had arrived from another planet Dortenmann and Fred Gross were staring at me.

A roar of laughter brought me to my senses. Red faces gasped for air trying to get their breath, heads shaking with uproarious laughter. I was standing on the steps of the canteen in Versailles and it was only a few minutes past five.

★ ★ ★

Long Patt was crowing and his protruding ears seemed to waggle continuously. He had a peculiar way of laughing. Anyone who watched him was highly amused by his natural comedy. He seemed to neigh and when he slapped his thighs you thought that you were in a Pomeranian inn with peasants drinking round after round of schnapps. His laughter would come from deep in his chest like a droning organ note, suddenly break off and, while his face muscles went on quivering, all you heard would be a dry whistling "hee, hee, hee!"

"Keep your trap shut. I can't take any more. Hee, hee, hee!" Sergeant Pilot Möller, a witty great chap from the Pfalz was telling his experience of the night before. He happened to be in the canteen and at a late hour was taken by the CO into a nearby room where the officers of the "*Grünherz*" were sitting round drinking heavily.

"Yes, we fellows from the Pfalz can be found all over the wide world." And he added, referring slyly to me, "I think we shall become good friends, that is if he doesn't forget that we're all jolly fellows in the Pfalz and that as soon as we've emptied our glasses we always get a bit familiar."

"What do you expect the poor devil to do if people keep on drinking to him because of his jump? He's obviously in the right mood for getting pissed."

"It's a bloody good job, boys, that you've no more flying to do today," said Fritz Kaluweit, who was fonder of the pilots than he would have been prepared to admit.

"You're right, Fritz. The Old Man can nurse his hangover. What do you think? Let's celebrate a few victories," suggested von der Jechten. "It's official that there's no flying today."

"That's great. The dustman will have a lot of work and when we break it up he won't know what to do with the 'dead men'. You'll have to give him a hand, Kaluweit. Well, start it up."

Möller took down the beribboned mandoline, a reminder of pre-war camping, and struck a few chords – Tum-tum-bingbong-bang!

" Oh give me a bright silver Focke.
Put the joystick right into my hand..."

the chorus rang out gaily. Patt imitated the bass violin. Von der Jechten drummed on a stool, Kaluweit grabbed a brush. Feet beat in time – sometimes softly, sometimes loudly... "*in a far-off fai-ry-land.*"

My arms round an imaginary partner, I began to waltz gaily round the room. The mood was very high that night among the pilots.

"The *Oberleutnant* shakes a pretty leg," said von der Jechten with admiration; and Möller added to this comment, "He's a natural gigolo. Just take a look how the old goose is swooning. If only the Old Man could see how smart this uniformed playboy from Montebello must have looked in civvies."

" You're dead right," I retorted. " It's just part of the fighter service that I bother to tell you what you can all do with yourselves. Why do you stand there grinning like a donkey, Kaluweit?"

"Oh, *Herr Oberleutnant*, I can assure you it's from pure admiration."

Chapter Four

THE ENEMY fought grimly for every square foot of soil. His losses were appalling. But this time even America had no consideration for her sons with whom she had hitherto been so sparing. British and Canadian crack regiments attacked our lines day and night. St Lô and Caen became the Verdun of the Second World War.

Unceasingly and brilliantly planned and well-organised supplies staff pumped new men and material into the bridgehead. One had the uncomfortable feeling that it was a boiling cauldron which might boil over at any minute. The pressure against the German pincers grew ever more dangerous.

Pluto pipe-lines on the pattern of those used in the Middle East oilfields were laid by special craft in the Channel and the fuel that is so vital in modern warfare flowed from England under the sea to the coast of Normandy. Not only were reinforcements brought by big troop transports, but large airborne landings increased the strength of the invasion troops. An umbrella of about 5,000 fighters protected the bridgehead. New airfields were built in a few hours. Gigantic bulldozers levelled a certain area; cunningly contrived steel matting built in sections provided practical runways for heavy aircraft. Barrage balloons were placed next to each other for miles on end making an impassable wall of sharp steel cables to protect vital supply points.

For several days airborne troops were dropped in great numbers from Skymasters in the St Lo area. Similar to the giant German troop-carriers used in 1940-1 in Russia, three gliders towed by an aircraft – usually a Bristol Blenheim – each carrying sixty to one hundred fully armed soldiers. Over the target the gliders were released and landed independently.

Orders were given to attack them.

The pilots found this the worst possible "bind". To penetrate this hotly defended stronghold needed great courage, and the mission was only ordered by the German High Command as a desperate measure; were the enemy to advance any farther eastwards and southwards in the Caen sector the Battle of Normandy would have been lost.

The Inspector of the Fighter Arm, *Oberst* Trautloft, appeared in person to address the assembled pilots. In the old days he had been in command of *Jagdgeschwader* 54 and, in memory of his Thuringian homeland, had given it a green heart as a symbol. The attack was to be carried out in three consecutive waves. He shook hands with everyone. The *Oberst* stopped for a moment in front of me. He had known me a year and a half before in Siwerskaya. My hand trembled nervously at my cap peak, then I stretched out my arm.... Hell! In the pleasure of seeing Trautloft again I had forgotten the new Nazi greeting. Was it really the pleasure of meeting him again which had made me confused or was it this impossible, infernal mission which was due to start within the next few minutes?

We left headquarters with white, drawn faces.

* * *

From 12,000 feet the "Ravens" swooped down in righthand turns on to the target. The black smoke balls of the ack-ack looked like puffs of cotton wool. With a sigh of relief we noticed that, so far at least, no enemy fighters were about; that would not last very long.

Forty Me 109s remained aloft as spotters.

Rabe Anton waded in. A steep dive... That must be St Lô down there. Directly behind the outskirts of the town stretched a broad field with a few gliders which had just been unloaded. The huge "ramps" at their tails lay open like sluice gates.

In a raging inferno of fire from every gun below, the Fockes sought their target. Fires... columns of flames... soldiers rushing desperately for cover...

"Zwilling to Rabe Anton. Look out! More gliders coming in from the north-west." The *Gruppen Kommandeur* climbed and waggled his wings. The *Gruppe* regrouped for a new attack. There were the Bristol Blenheims – three, . . five... six of them. Eighteen gliders in tow – some twelve hundred men, then.

What must the poor devils inside have felt like without parachutes in the face of the attacking Germans?

Hell! It was not so easy to get near them. Strong air cover was spread like a glittering fish-net above the gliders. The heaven was full of "crates".

A reassuring glance at the thick cumulus clouds which had piled up in a favourable mass – the funk-holes of the air.

"Rabe Anton calling. All of you on your target. Wade in from below and then break off to the east. Careful of the barrage balloons."

Full boost... The sweat stood out on the pilots' foreheads. This terrifying ack-ack. As in a giant fireworks display, fountains of tracers zigzagged across each other against a background of burning machines and white parachute silk.

Now the fighters were below the enemy.

Fire! Bullets cut their way into the fabric sides of the gliders. They must be creating havoc among the unprotected bodies of the closely-pressed soldiers inside.

All over.... Only two or three gliders went into a spin but two hundred and forty men had dived to their death. Mustangs flung themselves into the fray against the Fockes. A parachute unfolded and fluttered just ahead of my aircraft. I nearly caught the falling man in my propeller.

A reassuring silence meant safety and a pause for breath in the muck after the terrifying ack-ack barrage. Keep turning... that's right.

Aircraft level in the artificial horizon. The little ball in the turn-and-bank indicator rushes to one side, so the Focke is skidding. Opposite rudder... That's right, the ball rolls back slowly into the centre position. Mad confusion reigned over the intercom. One of the "Zwilling" *Gruppe* reported that he was baling out. He must have been a veteran if he could keep his nerve in that inferno and make his report.

In a flash it grew light as though ghostly hands had pulled back a curtain. The sun was blinding. The funk-hole was now behind. I looked round quickly and sighed with relief.

I was not alone as I had feared. At least a dozen Fockes and a few lost Me 109s were flying between myself and the clouds. Far below some Fockes were at grips with the Mustangs.

"Blast you, look out, you fathead!"

I had to pull up the nose like lightning The fellow who now took up his position quite calmly next to me had almost rammed me as he sped past below. Order was restored in the *Staffel*. To starboard an aircraft waggled its wings. It was Fred Gross.

The savage firing of the light ack-ack no longer reached us, but now one black puff after the other burst ahead – outsize snowflakes in a black storm. Change altitude.... Lose 300 feet and then climb 200.... A bright glow in the middle of the cluster of bursts and a Focke was blown to pieces by a direct hit.

Ahead of us, somewhat lower, was a balloon barrage. Like treacherous oxen in a thicket these sheer hanging balloons seemed to charge at the *Staffel*. Wade in... In a steep dive the tracers sped towards the fat sausages. Four balloons caught fire and tumbled out of the sky, leaving a long trailing tail of flame without smoke.

Boom! I gave a start. The engine spluttered and the needle on the rev. counter began to fall. An ack-ack hit. A slight pressure on the red knob near the magneto control . . that would eject the canopy. Undo the harness... A short tug on the stick and the aircraft ejected me from my seat.

Pull the parachute rip-cord. A hard painful jerk between the shoulder-blades and the trusty silken canopy rose proudly overhead in the breeze.

A wretched position to be in...

To be taken prisoner. Judging by the balloon barrage I could not yet be over the German lines but, thank God, a light wind was blowing from the west. Below me, a strip of forest glided slowly past, then some undulating hilly country wlth green meadows in between, long hedges and big ploughed fields....

There! The zigzag of trenches, earthworks, positions. British Tommies... I could make out their flat plate-like tin helmets quite easily.

Swish... Bloody swine. So it was right, these bastards did shoot at a helpless pilot hanging from his parachute. And then the earth... I tumbled head over heels into a shell-hole.

I must get out of my harness. I struck the quick-release box and the parachute fell off. No one had arrived yet. The machine-gun shots grew louder... the swift crackle of the "Hitler saws" replied.

Would no one appear?

I crawled carefully up the side of the crater. Wait. Get down.... I need the parachute. I was an old hand at this now.... Once more I climbed up the side of the shell-hole and carefully pushed the parachute over the edge. That's it... Ugh! Arse over head in the mud. A fine predicament. When I examined the parachute I found that there were a dozen holes in it.

So I've fallen between the lines. The thought went round and round in my head. In no-man's-land. The sun's right overhead. So it's a long time until nightfall, unless they take me prisoner in the meantime..

⋆ ⋆ ⋆

I was not taken prisoner.

I had known the war from all sides – Poland, France and Russia had seen to that – but this was something quite new for me. While I lay in my shell-hole, with the parachute as a pillow, and looked up at the sky I recalled a host of bright memories: that ticklish job at Jarzevo; the railway bridge at Novosokoluik where, on a vital reconnaissance, I had lain for two hours under heavy shellfire and could neither go forwards nor backwards; Welikije-Luki, where my battalion had been surrounded in a Russian counter-attack and had been nearly wiped out. For five long days and nights – an agonising eternity of long hours without food, and utterly exhausted – I had lain under my dead comrades, with one bullet remaining in my revolver for the last eventuality.

And then Rshew, 40° below, without winter uniform, crossing a railway bridge over the Volga... 30 per cent casualties from severe frost-bite. The building of the bridge was completed after four terrible weeks of indescribable privation and then it had to be blown up once more by our own men before the Russians crossed it...

And now I lay there like a silent observer on the fringe of the war... This whining, screaming and whistling up there did not concern me... An exchange of shots in a tennis match.

And I lay between the two fronts.

The luminous hands of the service watch on my left wrist showed midnight. A bright starlit June night. At last the treacherous moon slipped behind a bank of clouds. It would not be hidden for long, for the cloud was not very thick.

Make it snappy, Heilmann.

I had had plenty of time to take my bearings. The compass hanging at my belt had at last proved to be of some use. An hour ago I had seen gun flashes from the small copse over there. They must have been from a German artillery position. In their direction about fifty yards away lay a ruined farm. I made my way towards its dark shadow. Using every available piece of ground cover I crawled and ran through the night. Ugh! How hot it was in this flying suit.

I reached the farm. Now I was under cover. Careful... A soft "Hello". No reply. "Hello!" Nothing... Once more...

A dark strip of wood loomed up broad and threatening ahead of me like a black wall. Damn it! Now the moon was coming out again. No matter, press on! A hedge ran in a favourable direction and I was able to make use of it. The ground here was overturned as if a giant's plough had been at work. Shell holes gleamed in the cold hostile moonlight... a crater landscape of strangling death. A nauseating sickly sweet smell of blood pervaded the cool night air. The battlefield...

A flare hissed high into the sky and every detail of the battlefleld was outlined in its greenish-white magnesium light. A machine-gun immediately spat. The shots lashed the night. I was covered with earth. Get under cover...

In desperation I crouched in a small rut. They must have spotted me... Now the British replied. A bloody business...

I must have lain there for a quarter of an hour before the firing ceased. A few more single shots and then silence returned to no-man's-land.

"Hello... *Kameraden*!"

What the hell was that? An excited rustle... I made my way slowly towards the sound. After the recent exchange of shots, I no longer dared to stand up. And then voices close to me... A hand grabbed my arm and pulled me into a shallow trench.

"Are you the pilot who bailed out this afternoon?"

"We thought it was a Tommy."

They took care of me.

"So it was you who were shooting at me just now, was it? Well, take me to your headquarters. I'm *Oberleutnant* Heilmann of the III./JG 54."

Barely half an hour later I was in a lorry on the way to Nantes. The roads were in a turmoil. Only by night could reinforcements be brought up. During the day the fighter-bombers were masters of the sky.

I sat dozing next to the driver. My shoulders ached from the opening of the parachute.

"Here we are, sir."

Nantes. The soldiers' canteen was still open. An uncomfortable spot. The acrid smell of stale beer and tobacco smoke; all over the tables butt ends and matches for which there was no more room in the already full ashtrays....

I sat down in a dark corner on a bench, stuffed my parachute pack under my head and immediately fell asleep.

On the following morning I found a car to take me to Paris. I telephoned immediately to the fighter *Gruppe*.

"Villacoublay, please, for *Oberleutnant* Heilmann."

I got no further. There was a cry of pleasure at the other end of the line.

"Who's speaking?"

"Ah, *Herr* Heilmann. It's good to hear you. This is Lene Mersen. Don't you recognise my voice?"

Of course I did. It was Hannes Möller's little dark-haired girl with the saucy eyes and the antics of a kitten which knows how to use its claws. So Montebello also had an information service.

"Hanschen will be so pleased. Your boys took such a beating last night... So few of them..." There was an embarrassed silence. "I'll call Villa."

"Villa here. *Gefreiter* Kiks speaking."

I reported my arrival and asked for a car to be sent to pick me up at St Denis, where I was waiting in a brasserie.

The losses were appalling. From my *Staffel* 7 in particular: *Leutnant* Knebe in Clichy hospital with burns; von der Jechten had over fifty holes in his "crate" and was suffering from scratches and splinter wounds. Venjakob, the smart *Gefreiter* from Bonn with the highest number of victories in the *Gruppe*, was missing. Missing, too, were *Oberleutnant* Kupferberg, the untidy Frankfurter with the mop of red hair – this was his first operational flight after a tedious convalescence – and two *Gefreiter*s who had been sent straight from home.

Leutnant Venners from *Staffel* 9 was in Clichy with broken legs (crash-landing after being hit just behind his own lines). He had been with me for the past six months in the West Fighter *Gruppe* in Biarritz and then in Markisch-Friedland. We had shared a hut and were close friends.

Seventy per cent of the "*Grünherz*" aircraft were out of action and over half the pilots who had taken part were out of it.

* * *

Fritz Kaluweit looked grave when he served the meal to his "youngsters". We were trying to make up a four at skat but it was no good. Patt flung the cards down angrily on the table. Bert Venjakob had been his best friend.

"Let's scrub it," I said. "It's too difficult to concentrate. Your nerves won't let you..."

The four of us went on sitting there: Patt, Möller, Anderl Gusser, a black-bearded Tyrolean whose beard was always getting him into trouble because he needed an exceedingly sharp razor-blade, and myself.

"Now they'll have to give us a few days' rest whether they like it or not."

"Do you think so, Hannes?" I said, looking dubiously at the man from the Pfalz.

The others shook their heads with resignation.

"It couldn't matter less to those bastards back there. You've got to report carrying your head under your arm if you want to be left in peace," grumbled Patt.

"Well spoken. They have thick heads, those bloody 'scrambled eggs'." Hannes Möller pushed the table back, stumbled to his feet and turned on the wireless. "Didn't you know Surgeon Sauerbruch has got a lot of wooden heads all ready for you?"

Chapter Five

REINFORCEMENTS arrived – twenty pilots, of whom seven were officers. All of them were mere boys and their pale faces betrayed that they knew what lay ahead of them. Another dozen destined for the "*Grünherz*" were waiting in Cologne. *Leutnant* Wirz, who had ferried them, was in a raging temper with the Cologne factory. Hundreds of Fockes stood on the airfield waiting for the Boeings or Liberators but they could not get thirty-five of them airworthy for a quick take-off.

Wirz had come from the Baltic where the remains of the two fighter *Gruppen* of the former Trautloft *Geschwader* were stationed. He was an old *Staffelkapitän* from II *Gruppe* and was not very pleased to exchange the East for the invasion front. There was still good hunting there with superior machines – and, besides, the Russian air tactics were usually harmless. For that reason, in the East one needed about a hundred kills to win the Knight's Cross, but here in the West twenty sufficed.

Wirz gave a description of conditions in Berlin. He had looked up his old commanding offlcer, who was now an Inspector on the Fighter General Staff. He was lucky to find him, for *Oberst* Trautloft, like his chief, *Generalmajor* Galland, spent very little time in Leipziger Strasse 7. Wirz managed to get hold of him.

"Well, you old hell-hound, how are you getting on?" asked the jovial square-headed *Oberst*, slapping him on the shoulder. He had taken Wirz in his car for a few hours on a tour of inspection to Rechlin, the test station which had the reputation of sabotaging the first-class designs of our aircraft designers by turning them into heavy "crates" on the excuse of military expediency.

Wirz now related his experiences. At last he began to speak of personal matters and mentioned the name of the *General Luftzeugmeister*. His audience learned for the first time that *General* Udet had suffered the same fate as Werner Mölders.

All the pomp and ceremony of a state funeral.... Dust was being thrown in the eyes of the people. An irreplaceable hero had given his life for Germany and a ruthless fiend had driven him to commit suicide. The pilot who cannot find death in an air battle takes a revolver or a phial of poison. *Generalmajor* Galland was the leader of the six highranking officers who, with drawn swords, kept watch over Udet's coffin. Later he said to Trautloft that he nearly vomited when the real murderer laid his ostentatious wreath on the grave.

★ ★ ★

The new machines were made airworthy at feverish speed. All the FW 190s were checked from nose to tail. On the test and work benches rudder and engine components and idiosyncrasies, radios, superchargers and weapons were checked and rechecked. The needles on the instrument panel had to react correctly and fast.

My senior NCO, *Stabsfeldwebel* Michel, and I wandered around between the machines in earnest conversation. A host of brand-new Fockes had arrived and some of the "crates" had to be hidden in the pinewood. The fighter *Gruppe* was now better equipped than it had been at the beginning of the invasion.

My two mechanics in greasy overalls were overhauling a new Focke which I myself had flown an hour before. A slight alteration to the rudder bar was necessary. A painted White I had already been sprayed in front of the black cross.

The parachute officer suddenly ran over to us reporting that a readiness signal had just come through. I was wanted on the telephone.

I covered the thirty yards in record time to the *Oberfeldwebel*'s office.

The Adjutant was on the phone.

"Heilmann. Strong formations of four-engined bombers are on their way to Paris. Get all the new machines as quickly as possible under cover. All airworthy machines must get into the air at once. Fly low and assemble with the Chartres group. From there an attack will be made on the bombers.

"OK, Neumann."

The sirens wailed and the airfield sprang into activity.

The unchecked machines were quickly taxied away. Pine branches were placed on the wings and two or three small trees placed crosswise to protect the engines.

Staffel 9 roared over the field in waves of six or eight machines. They had been parked in a favourable position right on the flarepath next to *Staffel* 8, which took off after them. It was a strange sight for the raw pilots with no war experience. On the home airfields the station commander dealt out heavy punishments and threats of court martial, but here one took off at top speed from the edge of the field, the start signal being given by red and green flares.

Two machines from *Staffel* 7 took off. Möller taxied fast past my dispersal pen; I was still waiting for my parachute. The *Oberfeldwebel* had to switch me to another machine which was ready for flying. Möller braked so hard that his tail rose in the air and he nearly stood on the nose. What was wrong? Red flares were being fired. No more take-offs....

Möller jumped out of his machine and flung himself in a shell-hole. The next moment there was a whine and a rattle of machine-gun bullets. Yellow tracers hit his Focke... A mushroom of fire rose in the air.

Thirty Mustangs suddenly roared over the airfield like a poisonous swarm of angry hornets.

Low-level attacks. A quick rush for cover... A Focke crashed in flames into the deep narrow valley to the west of the airfield.

The bomber stream...

A wild rush began. Men tumbled head over heels into the dug-outs which had been built into the walls behind the hangar. The last mechanics and pilots jostled each other in twos and threes to get into the small fox-holes between the pens.

I tumbled over my leading mechanic.

Close-pressed, we gasped for breath, our hearts beating anxiously. Every man for himself...

The pathfinders sent down their cascades of white and red flares. The Christmas tree was lit. At last they knew. The attack was directed at Villacoublay.

And then above the heavy drone of the Boeings we could distinguish a soft, hissing swish swelling to a wild wail... infernal thunder and explosion. The earth shook beneath the hammer blows. Flames, smoke, the sharp whistle of shrapnel.... Whole aircraft wings, undercarriages and tail units were flung into the air and a rain of smashed fragments was strewn over the tortured ground. The earth quaked beneath an apocalyptic flail.

This hellish storm, which lasted a bare quarter of an hour seemed like an eternity. When at last it was over and from all sides trembling hands brought aid, trying to rescue sooty sweating figures, the whole northern edge of the airfield had changed its face – ploughed up and smashed to pieces.... Where once green pines had invited one to a summer siesta there was now an impassable jungle of torn and splintered tree-trunks with the green foliage dripping an oily black. Destroyed aircraft, burning oil, blazing petrol stores and broken human bodies....

The barracks of *Staffel* 7 were burning fiercely. Twenty yards away in a chaotic heap lay a pile of Fockes and the wreck of a Boeing. Almost within reach outside my foxhole were the remains of an American who had baled out and whose parachute had "torched". He had been squashed flat like a counterpane – a bloody pulp with every bone broken.

* * *

At the briefing which followed immediately we realised that we had come through well. The pens of *Staffeln* 8 & 9 were undamaged as well as the chateau which served as headquarters, mess, kitchen and offices for the

Gruppe staff. There were few bomb-holes on the runway itself, but the northern edge and the groups of houses in the vicinity had been flattened for two miles. *Staffel* 7 had been completely wiped out – aircraft, parachute and spare-part stores, fuel tanks and huts, also several of the hangars and buildings of the ground staff situated on that side of the airfield.... The hardest blow was the destruction of the expensive and irreplaceable workshops where over thirty aircraft were being repaired.

One piece of luck. The deep dugout had stood up to the attack. Nearly a hundred men had been saved from the clutches of death but about a dozen were killed in their foxholes and twenty-five airmen were wounded.

Was it by chance or did the enemy know that the "*Grünherz*" had just been re-equipped?

The latter presumption was the more probable and only some mysterious trick of fate had allowed the carpet of bombs to fall 2,000 yards too far to the north.

The first Fockes returned.

The concrete runway had received a few direct hits. Four holes were carefully marked with red flags.

The two aircraft of *Staffel* 7 taxied round looking in vain for their pens. They were diverted to *Staffel* 8. The *Gruppen Kommandeur* hurried with the officers who had landed to headquarters, where they met others in their filthy mudstained uniforms.

"That was one in the eye for us, gentlemen," said Weiss, looking gravely at our grimy faces. "Who crashed over there in the valley near the railway?"

No one knew. In the general excitement no one had thought to go and have a look.

"Hadn't you tuned in your RT, Heilmann?"

"No, sir. I never got off the ground."

"Lucky fellow," laughed Weiss. "I saw the first fighters coming and popped off the red flares like mad so that anyone who hadn't taken off could taxi away. It was crazy," he said turning to Dortenmann, "for your lot to start. How did you get out of it?"

Dortenmann gave his report.

He had been concentrating on his take-off. A green flare had just given him the OK and he was roaring with his eight machines along the runway before he heard Weiss's siren wail. It was too late, so they took off and hedge-hopped without being spotted by the Mustangs.

"And then you called me, sir, and I stayed where I was and could see the circus right under us."

"High time, too, old boy," said Robert Weiss, slapping the young *Leutnant* on the shoulder. "And I've got to thank you, too. When the Mustangs saw the new enemy streaking down from above most of them turned tail and scarpered. Although they were three times superior in numbers the fellows up there seemed to be a bit windy."

Hauptmann Lang came in at that moment. "A bloody business, eh, Robert?"

A young officer sprang to help him out of his flying suit. "You look like chimney-sweeps," said Bully, laughing at the staff officers. "Believe me," he went on, "I enjoyed myself up there, in spite of my sparring partner, when I recognised the black column of smoke and the fountains of fire on Villa."

"Everything's all to hell in your part of the field, Heilmann. Be honest, Robert. Old Lang always warned you that *Staffel* 7 lay too far away from the field. How often did they join us far too late?"

"The main thing, Emil, is that they've lost no pilots. Let's hope the missing ones return, including that poor sod over there in the valley. Did any of you actually get to Chartres?"

No one...

And it turned out to be just as well. They were informed of drizzle in the district; the Chartres aircraft could not take off, making it impossible for them to send any help to Villacoublay.

Chapter Six

SO LIFE went on and with it the struggle. Day after day the crews flew against the enemy... Two missions a day, sometimes more. The veterans who had only been a short time on the invasion front managed to get through somehow and the newcomers – most of them mere boys – were already veterans after two or three scraps with the enemy. It was seldom that any of them got through to the tenth dog-fight. There were pilots among them who let themselves be shot down without taking any avoiding action or without even firing back. "Target flying", the *Gruppen Kommandeur* called it. As though hypnotised, the newcomers flew straight into the enemy tracers.

The old hands did everything in their power to jolt the youngsters out of their coma. At favourable moments, when there were no enemy aircraft about, Weiss ordered practice flights over the airfield. Split-arse turns just above the ground were the tactics here. Some of them caught on and flew well, but when it came to a dog-fight they became once more a prey to that deathly frozenness, that helplessness which can only be attributed to panic sown among these young inexperienced fellows at the appearance of the superior enemy *Staffeln*.

Unforgivable faults had been committed at the training stations. Typical spit-and-polish routine with no knowledge of human psychology. The young men, when they left, were warned to keep a stiff upper lip, for, on the invasion front, statistics showed that a German fighter remained operational for only five hours and that the pilot's life was limited to about four weeks.

It was therefore the whole spiritual approach which made these newcomers weaken. Flying accidents only claimed a limited number of victims.

On the *Kommandeur*'s orders I addressed the men between flights. "Soul-searching", Neumann called it. Forcefully and without disguising my resentment at the daily losses, I would say, "The first and foremost thing is for you to stick it out. Stick ruthlessly to the chaps with experience. Any straggling or intentional evasion means your death. Above each air battle you will find experienced sections – in our case, *Hauptmann* Lang likes to do this himself – on the watch for a formation to break up, for then they get a sitting target. You are not experienced and adaptable enough to shake off an enemy who is diving on you with all the advantages of height."

The newcomers were grateful for this advice, but in the next air battle they forgot it and once more death reaped a rich harvest.

⋆ ⋆ ⋆

"If we can't influence those silly bastards at the training station we must put our cards on the table and tell the *General* of this swinish position."

Hauptmann Weiss was growing bitter.

"I feel so terribly responsible when I have to look on and see these poor sods being shot down, and yet I can't spare them. Only yesterday the *Oberst* gave me a rocket because I had put too few machines into the air. Apart from the fact that in the long run I can't let the novices off and go up with a few veterans on my own or else some nitwit will be on my trail and then I'm in the cart... Sabotaging the strength of the formation. It hasn't yet been decided whether or not we shall one day become an SS *Staffel*." (He was thinking of the consequences of the 20th July.[1]) Weiss turned resolutely to me. "Look, what you've told me I shall pass on without pulling my punches. Make out a full report which I can send through Trautloft to the *General* of the fighters. Do it at once."

⋆ ⋆ ⋆

While the *Gruppe* took off on another mission I sat in the next room dictating on the typewriter:

"On orders from the Officer Commanding III./*Jagdgeschwader* 54, I beg to give the following report on Fighter Group Training Station Bad V... to which I was attached from the 6. I I .43 to 9.5.44

1. *Period of waiting*

The pilots who have graduated from the 'A' schools have to wait on an average six months before they can be given any flying training. I know of individual cases where soldiers who had been with the group for a year had never flown since leaving 'A' school.

2. *Tuition*

The whole tuition is completed over a period of four weeks, seven to ten hours daily. On account of the subsequently described conditions, gravely harassed soldiers were not in the position, in a ten-hour daily session, to grasp intelligently the enormous scientific field covered.

Firing, arms instruction and sundry technical subjects were insufficiently well taught. For example, in the case of air combat, apart

[1] 20th July 1944 – the attempt on Hitler's life.

from a few important classic routine manccuvres, additional subjects relative to this were handled too cursorily (e.g. What are the duties of a *Staffel* orderly-room clerk?). Hour-long lectures were entirely wasted cataloguing individual officer's duties. Aircraft recognition, on the other hand, a very important subject – and at this moment of invasion of the greatest importance – had to be completed within a few hours. In spite of the expert knowledge of the instructor officers and with the best teaching methods, 90 per cent of the training group could not follow the tuition.

3. Flying training

Flying training was good, particularly in III *Gruppe* (*Leutnant* B...). After the bombing of the Training School at Bad V... on 1.4.44 and its transfer to N..., *Leutnant* M..., *Kapitän* of *Staffel* 1, was given command of the *Gruppe* while the *Kommandeur* took over a hotel in V...

At this time the training was considerably better organised, and despite the bombing and the resultant difficulties many more pupils were turned out.

4. Organisation and leadership. Esprit de corps

As an officer still under training I had more opportunity to be with the men than the other officers of the group. During my whole time of service as a soldier since 1938 – even during the most critical days of the war – I have never seen soldiers who carried out their duties with so little pleasure and with so much compulsion. Pilots are volunteers and are therefore to a great extent men of excellent physique and character. That the soldiers of the *Jagdgeschwaderen* are so lacking in military qualities I attribute to the following reasons: the six-month period of waiting is a very great hardship for young men who are being trained as pilots. To this must be added a completely irrational treatment. From morning till evening, day after day, they have ground duties. The work on an airfield is of course very considerable but could nevertheless easily be handled with proper planning. One example of this was that, in view of the numbers available, most of the exercises had to be cancelled because there was so much work and so few people! There was also far too little sport.

There was an hour's break at midday. It was never observed. I myself was present when *Leutnant* N..., at that time *Staffelkapitän* of *Staffel* 1, was given a heavy rocket over the telephone by the *Kommodore* because he had permitted a whole hour break. ('Kindly get it into your head that half an hour is quite sufficient!') The *Kommodore* must have known that the men would hardly have time to gulp down their meal in half an hour. In practice, men doubled to the messroom, stood nervously round the hot-plate and swallowed their meal... and fell in again on parade. A few of the airmen naturally came too late in such a frantic rush. This made a further shortening of the break.

Unfortunately the airmen took it into their heads to skip lunch. They were found eating in their huts. After this their quarters were locked from early morning and only opened again late in the evening after duties. A few airmen continued to slip through the windows and so, on the personal orders of the *Kommodore*, numerous openings to the huts, including cellars, were sealed up with boards. Several windows on the ground floor were even nailed up.

It is easy to understand the mood of the pupils. The mess parties, dances and suppers (which should be a matter of course in any body of troops), even when the men got the necessary permission, only lowered the mood and, in individual cases, increased the hatred of the pupils. Tickets for the theatre were only issued to officers, and the NCOs were only given an occasional ticket for the circus. After the bombing and the transfer to N... food supplies were totally inadequate (service from four in the morning until ten at night, with a plate of soup at midday – no second courses). Dr M... pointed out at a conference that the constant physical overstrain could not last much longer. Previously in this connection an order had been in force whereby a pilot was immediately placed under arrest when he declared that for physical reasons he was incapable of flying. (*Leutnant* v C... admitted this to Dr M... in my presence in my quarters.)

In the Officers' Corps the *Kommodore*, *Major* M..., was unpopular and his behaviour and regulations were bitterly criticised. Neither the *Gruppen Kommandeur* nor the three *Staffelkapitaen* were allowed to make their own decisions. *Major* M... quoted his seniority on every possible occasion. Characteristic was his remark to the Officers' Corps: 'Gentlemen, I ask no more of you than I myself have done in the past.'

On the other hand, he called a briefing and when an officer tried to reach him on the telephone at eight o'clock in the morning he maintained that it was quite unheard of that subalterns should disturb their superior's early-morning sleep.

Such things were common knowledge throughout the whole *Gruppe*; they were exaggerated and repeated until remarks were attributed to the *Kommodore* such as: 'Mess night is far more important than night-flying ops.'

I have constantly mentioned in officers' circles that those in command lacked experience and that there was no conception of the right way to treat men and certainly not how to train soldiers. The treatment of these volunteers in their fifth year of the war is nothing less than a crime."

Chapter Seven

August 3rd, 1944

BRIGHT blue summer sky lay over Normandy; a day so little in harmony with the obstinate bloody struggle 1 being waged in the front lines.

In the early hours of the morning the British attacked Caen. Our lines were broken but the SS panzer division "*Hitlerjugend*" closed the ring. It was wiped out. The "*Grünherz*" had already flown their third mission. Their target was the troops trying to break through to the east of Caen. Low-level attacks were carried out with rocket-firing cannons which were used for the first time – two cannon beneath each wing. Tanks were blown up, mass attacks were dispersed and artillery positions put out of action.

The enemy fighter defence was particularly strong that day, but the most dreaded opponent, the fast, well-armed Spitfire, was not so much in evidence. Not a single Tempest, which was 50 mph faster, was to be seen. The V-1 had lifted a great weight from our minds. England must have thrown in practically all her fighter strength on the defensive against the German pilotless aircraft in Southern England.

The Americans were far easier game. Unless they were in enormous superiority they lacked the Englishman's bulldog persistence. Mustangs and Lightnings were in any case no match for the Focke – provided it was flown by an able pilot.

Only the Thunderbolt at great height was something of a headache. It had a high altitude engine with a turbo-supercharger which gave it a tremendous performance. Nor could one dive away from this Thunderbolt; its enormous weight combined with powerful engines allowed it to dive like a stone and to overtake the German machines in the shortest possible time.

A few "bulges" (Me 109s) and two *Staffeln* of Fockes were having a scrap between 3,000 and 1,000 feet with some Mustangs when the "*Grünherz*" waded in to the attack. The target was a concentration of tanks. *Staffel* after

Staffel broke off and dived on them. Rocket explosions... machine-guns... mushrooms of flame with jet-black whorls of smoke...

Now *Staffel* 7 was over the target. I half-rolled away to port followed by my "winger". Flight after flight followed. The tanks milled around trying to escape. They were too late. I had one of the black giants in my sights. I pressed the tit. A slight tremor ran through the machine indicating that the rockets had gone.

Leaving a long comet tail behind them, they hissed down to the target. Boom! A direct hit!

Hedge-hopping in a cauldron of ack-ack fire... altitude regained... a half-roll and a new attack from the opposite direction. This time the machine-guns wreaked havoc among the English positions. There to the right... a gun emplacement, and behind it three of the typical armour-plated shields.

Wade in...

The gunners ran for their lives. Sprayed by the bullets, they flung themselves on the ground; their flat tin helmets rolled all over the place.

That was silly of you, boys. You were safer behind your steel plates. But you could not possibly know that the "Jerry" had no more bombs or rockets under the belly of his "crate".

New targets were sought, recognised and strafed. They must have suffered heavy casualties below...

A burning Mustang spun through the circus of the attacking Fockes. Not far away from its burning debris an Me 109 made a crash-landing.

Tough luck, old man! You'll probably break all your teeth... Pity! Had you been flying in the other direction you might have landed behind our lines...

The attack had to be broken off. The shot-counter on the instrument panel showed that there was no more ammo left.

Hedge-hopping on a southerly course. The ack-ack left a trail of tracers behind us... Too late. The "birds" hopped over hedges and villages.

I was now alone with my *Staffel*. The others were still in action when I reported over the RT.

We sped southwards above the tree-tops at 350 mph I grinned as I saw the panic our appearance caused. So near the ground no one could distinguish a German from an Allied machine when it suddenly bobbed up and roared over.

Everyone ran for cover – German soldiers, Normandy peasant women, men and cattle... Horses broke into a wild gallop, cars pulled up and their occupants dived quickly into the ditch.

Suddenly my Focke came under fire from the right and a German flak battery now succeeded in doing what the Tommy had not achieved that day with my *Staffel*. My neighbour plunged into a wood. Gain height... Drop a red flare... The firing ceased, for the gunners had recognised the black crosses.

We flew in a wide circle round this fatal copse. No smoke was to be seen at the scene of the crash. Then we discovered the path that the Focke had hacked out... over a hundred yards long. At the end of it lay the machine.

Soldiers were attending to the pilot, who was lying on the ground near the wreckage.

He seemed to have got away with it...

The pilot must have put his machine down in the pine tops which had acted as a brake as the powerful wings had cut them off.

On the following day *Feldwebel* Pilot Knell, with a parachute under his arm, limped into Villa. It was a miracle. Apart from some bruises and a badly grazed shinbone he had suffered no damage, but the shock could still be seen in his tortured eyes.

* * *

Hmm! That does you good... "I feel as cannibally well as five hundred sows," I muttered, remembering a famous quotation. Another shower... hot... cold... brrr...

Shaking myself like a wet dog, I sprang out of the bath tub. I dried my wet body, rubbed myself with a coarse towel until my whole body was as red as a lobster. A look into the mirror... Ah, you ape! One of us must have a shave...

Whistling cheerfully, I reached for my razor, loosening up my muscular legs like an athlete. It's not decent that I should always be whistling English soldiers' songs like *It's a long way to Tipperary*, but what the hell! Why doesn't Herms Niel write something decent for us instead of his old-fashioned collection of sloppy girls' names? And that damned nostalgic tune: *Ich möht zu Fuss na Kölle gahn*... it's too bloody stupid, and not only on account of the line "Throw away your arms".

Well, there we are. You look smashing, old man.

I pranced back to my room.

Do you fancy me like this? I winked at a photograph of my wife that stood on the table. You ought to be ashamed of yourself. Look the other way when a man's getting dressed. I put the photo face downwards. Women always made things so difficult...

The mild evening air made me feel so good. I just wanted to lie idle in front of the window, looking at the green forest drive leading to the airfield.

One felt so clean and innocent after all the sweaty, oilsmeared tasks of the day.

Thoughtfully I lay down on the couch and poured myself out a brandy.

There was a knock on the door.

"Wait a moment." I gulped down my drink, put on my training shorts and white polo shirt. Where the hell had Max hidden my sandals again? Naturally right under the bed just where I couldn't get at them. Then I opened the door.

"Evening, Willi."

It was Hannes Möller. We had become close friends. The same country, the same blood... Our similarity of character had led to a genuine friendship such as is invariably born among those who are constantly flirting with danger and death.

"Make yourself at home, Hannes," I said, pushing forward a chair.

"What are you reading? Goethe. *Hermann und Dorothee*. Do you find that's the right sort of stuff to read here?"

"Take a look for yourself." I took the book from his hand, turned over a page or two until I found what I wanted. With my finger on the quotation I handed it back to my friend. "Here, you just read that."

And Hannes Möller, who, with his broad hands on the joystick, had gambled with death and destruction in a hundred dog-fights, read in a soft voice which one only heard when he was playing his beloved banjo:

Denn Alles bewegt sich jetzt auf Erden einmal:
es scheint sich Alles zu trennen...

The telephone rang and interrupted the silence that ensued.

"Yes. Heilmann speaking."

"Weiss here. Come with us to the Café de la Paix. We must have a farewell drink with Emil. He's been appointed *Kommandeur* of *Gruppe* III, *Jagdgeschwader* 26 and has to leave tomorrow morning."

* * *

Half an hour later I locked my door.

"Are you coming with us, Hannes?"

"If the Commander doesn't mind."

The front door banged. Outside stood my Citroën. I started up the engine and the bright yellow sports car slipped through the narrow streets of Malabri and turned into the wide autostrade that led to Versailles.

"You drive too damned fast," said Möller, lighting a cigarette. He lit another and put it between my lips. "Don't drive like such a bloody lunatic. You're not in your 'crate' now."

I turned off sharp to the right. The twilit landscape slipped by: clusters of villas in small pine woods, well-tended parks and the small sloping valleys between St Germain and Sceaux, so typical of the Seine bank south of Paris.

We reached Jouy.

Taking a small tarred road on which it was impossible to turn between the sandstone walls of a large park, we pulled up outside our favourite meeting place.

It was a magnificent roomy house famous for its cuisine, an ideal place for an outing. At the back, from an enormous window, was a view over the broad misty countryside below – a view of Paris. A shady garden outside fenced by strong iron railings and below, falling 300 feet into the abyss, a slope covered with a mass of wild roses...

We were expected. Gaston, who was above all a business man and never uttered a word about politics, led us with obsequious bows through the restaurant, in whicl practically only Frenchmen were sitting, into the garden.

"Voila, meine 'erren – ! S'il vous plaît!"

It was getting late. A bright starry night spread its gleaming net over sleeping Paris. The "Herren" paid; 500-franc notes changed hands. One was never economical when a good friend was leaving. It was a magnificent farewell party, delicious appetising hors d'œuvres, a roast, a strawberry omelette, with Benedictine for dessert. White Burgundy which warmed the heart and loosened the tongue...

Once more, as had so often happened, it was the parting of the ways. A good pal was leaving the community. Bully was taking Fred Gross with him. They had flown well together and that is an important thing when you start flying with a strange *Geschwader*.

I took over Bully's *Staffel* and *Leutnant* Wirz was to take over *Staffel* 7.

"Well, all the best, and good hunting, Heilmann," said Lang as he left. "And keep your eyes skinned. *Staffel* 9 has had experts. It's been spoiled. And, to be perfectly frank, I haven't bothered very much about the internal ramifications."

The "*Grünherz*" had grown used to Bully's strident orders on the intercom in tough fights and his crazy turns to get into a good firing position, but now we had seen them for the last time. *Hauptmann* Lang, Knight's Cross with Oakleaves, and *Leutnant* Gross, Knight's Cross, fell on the invasion front during the last days of the break-through.

* * *

So I was now in command of *Staffel* 9. I had taken Patt and Hannes Möller with me and *Staffel* 7 was given some new officers to balance this.

Hauptmann Lang had spoken the truth. The ground staff of his *Staffel* were a disorderly and undisciplined rabble. The *Stabsfeldwebel* thought of nothing but the mademoiselles and usually carried about a dozen photographs of his girl friends around with him in his wallet. The non-flying officer (each *Staffel* had a ground officer to represent the *Staffelkapitän* in service matters) was, one might say, a nitwit.

On the other hand the pilots were all first-class. *Leutnant* Zeller, *Gefreiter* Brandt, *Oberfeldwebel* Schlafer, with Möller and Patt, were the mainstays of the *Staffel*. They were a finer bunch than *Staffel* 7 and they could all rely on each other.

Orderly room clerk Kiks was with them and on the *Gruppen Kommandeur*'s orders had hung on a blackboard small cards with the aircraft numbers and the names of the pilots. At this time only half the *Staffel* was flying on each mission and the *Oberfeldwebel* had been given a hint not to report too many machines as airworthy. This was not sabotage: it was essential.

Neither Weiss nor his *Staffelkapitaen* could be responsible for this crazy "death or glory" stuff. Mission followed mission and between the individual take-offs there was often hardly the time to fill up and take new ammunition on board. Nerves were stretched to breaking point.

And these accursed low-level attacks were constantly repeated. In these forays there were infinitely more losses than in dog-fights; in those at least you could defend yourself, fight for your life and wrestle with the enemy for a favourable position, whereas the pilot in a low-level attack was at the mercy of the ground controllers. Formation leader or newest recruit, you had to fly along a certain path constantly under fire, following the RT instructions. Course and altitude were rigidly laid down. And no one knew whether he would ever get back because the ack-ack did not distinguish between Commander and novice, between this or that machine.

And there was another consideration – "Gongs".

In an air battle recognition was certain. So many victories, so many points. With five to seven points one was automatically given the Iron Cross First Class and on the Western Front anyone who reached twenty points could be certain of a Knight's Cross.

On low-level attacks this was quite different. Irresponsible and exaggerated reports of success during the first years of the war had demanded some system of control so as to make fantastic claims impossible. When a shot-down aircraft was not found on the "deck" or the flak could lay claim to it, the reported victory was not recognised.

Each report of success had to be written in quadruplicate and sometimes months elapsed before it was officially recognised. Often decorations could not be bestowed because the fighter pilot had long since been killed and they had to be sent to his next of kin.

But to return to the low-level attacks. Who could testify to a success when the pilot, himself in a mad ack-ack barrage, was not in a position to make clear observations?

Decorations, of course, were not the alpha and omega – life was more important to each individual pilot – but they went well with the uniform and a naked tunic was not viewed particularly well by anyone.

Thus Weiss cunningly took the opportunity of getting out of one of these unpopular low-level attacks when Marauders were reported in the area west of Paris. He had already summed up these fast twin-engined bombers. None of the "*Grünherz*" had ever managed to shoot down one of these powerfully armed aircraft. A dozen of the veterans, the so-called experts, were briefed and told to take off.

Robert Weiss himself led the flight. I flew once more as his "winger". Dortenmann, Wirz, Teumer (who had just returned from hospital), Zeller, Möller, Patt, and Schlafer made up the rest of the party.

"Prima-donna" from the Eiffel Tower gave us our instructions and within five minutes the Marauders were reported at 9,000 feet, flying on a south-westerly course, north of Versailles. On their flank, well out of range, we climbed to the required altitude – 3,000 feet above them. In broad circular spirals we dived on our target. Attack from above to port and from astern.

800... 500... 300... 200 yards. Let them have it!

A magnificently-aimed rapid fire met the dozen Fockes. There were about thirty Marauders but this brisk defence fire was quite unexpected. It was like flying through the ack-ack from the ships at the mouth of the Orne.

We huddled, small and insignificant, behind our windscreens, keeping our target well in the cross-wires of our sights. With bated breath and tense nerves we listened to the dreaded rattle of the bullets on our own aircraft, ready at any moment to release the canopy and bale out. Anyone who wanted to be saved by parachute dared not hesitate for even a fraction of a second. Usually it was too late.

Good show! Six Marauders were on fire and three more had broken away with thick smoke pouring from their engines.

I watched a black smoke-trail coming from the leader's machine; and while the Fockes waded in from below the scattered Marauder formation, I warned Weiss over the intercom. The *Gruppen Kommandeur*'s machine was on fire. The cabin flew off and a few hundred feet below a parachute opened...

What an extraordinary situation, I thought. There are more parachutes in the air than machines. It looks like an airborne landing.

When I looked around for my own pals I noticed, to my amazement, that there were only three of them. To starboard Zeller in his Yellow 4, to port Patt, and a hundred yards astern another Focke catching us up. A white number. That must be Wirz or Teumer.

The Marauders had jettisoned their bombs and had broken off to the north. They were obviously afraid of further attacks – but this would have been crazy with only four fighters.

This mission was written up in the *Gruppe* log-book with the comment: "The experts must be allowed to let down their hair."

Weiss, Wirz, Dortenmann, Möller, Brandt and Sterten – the latter was flying his fifteenth mission; for outstanding bravery he had already been given the Iron Cross First Class and promoted to *Gefreiter* – were swaying down on their parachutes. Schlafer and a *Gefreiter* landed in open country near the scene of the battle with shot-up engines. A curious situation arose: the *Kommandeur*, with his five comrades who had jumped, captured a dozen Englishmen who had managed to escape from their burning machines.

Out of the whole party, including two crash-landings, no one had suffered any injury.

Chapter Eight

THE bloody battle on the invasion front had been decided. The Americans broke through on a broad front at Avranches on the west flank of the bridgehead and penetrated deeply towards Rennes without meeting any resistance.

It was ironical in the history of this battle that the successful breakthrough took place on what had been the calmest part of the front since the landing. The British and Canadians on the right wing had won a few miles at the cost of terrific casualties. The Vlassov army had easily held the Americans, who, with their backs to the sea, had launched occasional faint-hearted attacks with a view to sparing the troops. Only a misunderstanding – I shall refrain from speaking of sabotage and treachery – brought about a crack in the front line here. The troops under Vlassov fought magnificently, for only a victory of German arms could save their lives.

On the evening of the 5th August Vlassov received orders to move. He was transferred to another part of the Normandy front and the troops who were to relieve him were on their way.

For a whole day the German front at this spot was free of troops. Towards evening American reconnaissance troops were faced with a problem. On the night of the 6/7th August they launched a cautious attack. They sensed a trap, but on the following day, too, they found no opposition.

Not until they reached Rennes, sixty miles to the south, did they come up against the first weak resistance. A flak company, ludicrously small in comparision with the attackers, flung itself into the fray. Red-hot barrels fired to the last shot and in hand-to-hand fighting the encircled gunners held out for almost a day to the last man.

On the 7th August the German High Command under von Rundstedt had completely lost sight of what was happening in the West. Fighter *Staffeln* had to make reconnaissance flights.

At the same time *Staffeln* equipped with rockets and cannon strafed the advancing Americans.

At 18,000 feet the *Staffel* made a wide sweep over Avranches. There were twenty-five Fockes led by Teumer, deputising for the *Gruppen Kommandeur*. Black mushrooms of bursting ackack fired from position after position accompanied them.

The northern turning point was reached. The orders were to make a low-level attack on the Americans, coming in from the north.

That day I was a prey to dark forebodings.

The previous evening I had succumbed to a sentimental mood and had made every effort to banish my weakness with alcohol. At midnight I was still writing letters as though wishing to say farewell and kept staring at the pictures of my young wife and children which stood in their place of honour on my writing desk..

This accursed flying superstition...

The utter hopelessness of my existence as a pilot had never stood out so clearly before my eyes.

I knew that my turn would have to come. I had got away with it far too many times already. Each mission was a challenge to fate in the present weak position of the German fighter arm.

I had to control myself to the utmost as I climbed on to the wing of my faithful Focke and scrambled into the cockpit. The paint was still damp on the fuselage indicating my thirteenth victory... and this hundred times accursed and yet wholeheartedly believed flying superstition upset me so much on account of this thirteen that I felt that a line had already been drawn sealing my fate.

During the mission my overstrained nerves grew a trifle calmer. The sharp exhilaration of the senses somehow dulled the constantly recurring thought, but now at 18,000 feet over Avranches my anxiety returned in all its strength.

In order to see nothing as I dived into the murderous barrage I huddled in my seat watching the peaceful regular play of the altimeter. At each breath it seemed to be opening and shutting like a pair of lips as I lost height.

The ack-ack fire increased until it became a veritable hurricane.

It was a miracle that anyone could get out of this... A broad stream of black mushrooms marked the path of our flight through the blue, sunny, cloudless midday sky.

In terror, and yet fully aware that I was in the utmost danger, I flew on. A shell burst quite close to my cockpit. Pitch-black smoke swirled from a bright-red ball of fire. My Focke was flung into the air.

Almost unconsciously I realised that my cockpit was riddled.

My helmet was torn and was now only hanging by one strap on my right ear. I flung it off, for it was of no further use. A quick report over the intercom. No answer... Had my aerial been shot away?

The rev. counter was far below the regulation 3,500 rpm. It kept falling.

The engine coughed and spluttered.

With compressed lips I banked to the left. God be praised, no sign of smoke to be seen, so there was no need to bale out. Before each parachute jump the pilot is terrified. A terrible pressure constricts his heart and stomach, and makes his knees tremble. This fear is constant, for the high tail unit and wings can often trap the man as he jumps out, and break all his bones.

Lack of oxygen now became noticeable. The blood seemed to seethe in my brain. My fingers suffered from pins and needles and were painful. Breathing became more difficult and with open mouth I felt dizzy, eagerly trying to force the rare oxygen into my panting, painful lungs.

There, in the greatest peril, my body slumped forward against the belt, one hand desperately clutching the joystick, the other on the throttle, a violet blue veil passed before my eyes; the altimeter passed the 12,000 feet mark where from now onwards the air contained sufficient oxygen.

And then by some miracle the engine, doubtless from the increased intake of oxygen, began to pick up. The needle rose on the rev counter and the Focke climbed eastwards out of the enemy's grasp.

Perhaps I can get to Chartres, I thought. The danger had restored my sang-froid. If not, I must find some piece of flat ground to put my "bird" down on.

I was still only at 6,000 feet.

No chance of getting to Chartres. It was a painful thought, for I had no idea how far the Americans had advanced in the meantime. That morning they had wheeled and a frontal attack was now expected in the Paris region.

So what, flashed through my mind... They'll take me prisoner and there'll be no more questions. The war's over... if not today, then tomorrow. In any case it will be over in a month and the whole bloody thing's been in vain. Fighting, bloodshed, pain, and, worst of all, death... It couldn't matter less if I'm taken one day sooner or later like a dangerous pirate by the Yanks; if I get away with my life the future after this collapse is not worth a shrug of the shoulders...

A nauseating, suffocating odour of petrol fumes poisoned the air in the cockpit. I looked attentively at the three instruments so vital for my engine – rev counter, pressure and temperature gauges. The temperature was very high and the needle wobbled far above the danger mark.

Keep it up, old fellow. We shall soon be down.

To my surpise I noticed four fighters behind me. Could they be Me 109s? No. Then by their lines they must be Spitfires. They had become very rare in the air over France since the "doodle-bug" attacks had begun.

I was right. They were Spits, and I could recognise them clearly as they drew nearer. Press the RT button and report to the ground station. Bloody fool that I was, I had forgotten that the gadget was out of action. A fiery necklace of tracers shot past the cockpit. I took no evasive action, for the badly damaged Focke had not sufficient speed to try and shake the pursuers off. The British had probably noticed this and with their usual gallantry were not going to shoot down a helpless enemy. They probably intended to force me to land on one of their airfields; this counted as a highly daring exploit and was given twice the number of marks awarded for shooting down an enemy plane. The British of course had the same system of points for their "gong " system as the Germans.

The oval pointed wings with the red, white and blue circles drew quite close.

The Tommies found it difflcult to throttle back to my speed.

They were flying with their flaps in the take-off position so that they acted as air-brakes. To the right of my Focke, not thirty feet away – flew the British leader's aircraft. A curious thing that sometimes happened among fighter pilots. The Britisher waved to me and pointed over his shoulder indicating that I should turn back.

I did not react...

The British pilot threatened...

A shake of the head...

A burst of fire far ahead of my Focke and again the signal to turn back. You must come with us or else we shall shoot you down like a sitting duck.

I looked slowly to right and left. I must gain time. My right hand was already on the red lever in front of the windscreen. At the slightest danger... if one of the Tommies tried to get into firing position I would pull the lever, release the cockpit and bale out... but I must play for time so that I would fall in German territory.

The Britisher banged his forehead with his fist. His gesture seemed to say: You're crazy, you bloody Jerry. A badly damaged Focke which could fall to pieces at any moment against four Spitfires...

Then the enemy flight turned off to starboard and got into formation to attack and give me the *coup de grâce*.

I pulled the lever and with a crash the hood fell away. The wind screamed and roared round my head.

One of the four Spitfires roared by overhead. Automatically I pressed the firing button and from four barrels spurted the deadly charge – tracer, percussion, armour-piercing and incendiary – into the slim smooth silver fuselage ahead of me.

A burst of flame. An explosion...

A rain of burning debris spun earthwards.

That was a damned low trick, Heilmann.

It had been a pure reflex action on seeing this silhouette which, for a German fighter, represented the bitterest opponent. It had been lightning swift, almost subconscious.

Now I had had my chips.

In the next second I was out of my machine. Faster and faster I tumbled, somersaulting, my whole body straining to brake the fall. A tug at the ripcord and for the sixth time within four weeks I swayed down earthwards, the white canopy fluttering proudly in the wind.

The remaining three Spitfires circled me.

Are they going to fire at me while I'm hanging here defenceless on my 'chute, I thought with a shudder, in revenge for my lousy trick of shooting down their comrade?

But they were British and were fair-minded enough to recognise my desperate gesture in its true light. They even waved to me as I hung there in the air. Then they broke off and disappeared at low level over a strip of wood.

I was in the air again on the following day.

My *Staffel* 9 had suffered terribly in this low-level attack.

Leutnant Zeller, my friend from Voslau, Schlafer, Brandt and my old pal Hannes Möller, the cheerful creature from the Pfalz, had all fallen in the hellish battle.

We were already flying our third mission that day. On our way to the front the "Ravens" became involved in a bitter dog-fight to the rear of Lisieux. Thirty Thunderbolts coming out of the sun made a surprise attack on twenty Fockes. The "*Grünherz*", sweating profusely, fired like maniacs. Smarting eyes stared into the sights. The ruthless hunt had already been on for nearly ten minutes.

This time it was a gruesome battle. No quarter was given on either side. The initial superiority of the Yanks was counter-balanced by skilfully flown tight-turn actions, and now the last machines – there were only about ten Thunderbolts and as many Fockes – were fighting so bitterly that no one could leave the fray. A German machine was hit by a spinning Thunderbolt. Two columns of smoke showed where they had crashed. Several more machines had crashed in a village which was now enveloped in a bright sea of flames.

In a sharp avoiding action I received a number of direct hits; once more I was hanging on my parachute and was forced to leave my burning Yellow 1 to its fate.

Hardly had the parachute opened than it was caught in the slipstream of a Thunderbolt's propeller. The silk and the cords "torched".

I fell like a stone, faster and faster, in a crazy dive earthwards. This was the end...

It must be like this when a condemned man stands before the muzzles of a firing squad. Seconds become the martyrdom of eternity.

And while my whole life seemed to pass before my eyes like a kaleidoscope I sped, a doomed man, towards my death.

It was terrible to see everything so clearly. In those moments, actually only a few seconds, everything passed before me. My own words seemed to mock me, words I had used at the grave of fallen comrades or in letters to my family, and an infernal echo drummed in my ears: "In the best years of his life... a true husband and loving father to his young children." Bloody rubbish. No one at home had the slightest idea of the unspeakable savagery with which the war pursued you until you were destroyed. The death of a hero? What else remained to you? A loathsome lump of pulp in a crushed uniform spat from the rage of the crash like a bloody gob.

Strange. In this utmost danger you forget to be afraid. You are not merely a spectator at this tragic sacrifice. Oh no. You know quite clearly that it is a question of your own survival or destruction, but all anxiety vanishes when you have fully realised that you're crashing to your death. It is as though the spirit is transformed into an unknown something, transcending the previously-experienced, as though the body released from feeling loses the knowledge and reactions of its nerves. Yes, that was right, the warmth, living warmth, for now you were cold and numb from the terrible shock of approaching death. A flutter and a loud report above my head made me look up. A miracle. The parachute had opened.

Suddenly the warmth of life streamed back with the overpowering feeling of being rescued. Dripping with sweat and once more in control of my nerves, I was hanging by my straps.

It was too much. This appalling overstrain on the nerves was unbearable for any man, and after all I was a man. Yes, a man, all the same, with a recognised goal although it was not so easy to shake off the long and bitter efforts of those long war years. So far and no farther. Whoever dares to exceed the invisible barriers of his own capacities must expect his nerves to let him down, and it is not very far to the next step into the eternal gloom of a living death, madness.

I had snapped as I realised that I was a defenceless victim condemned to plummet like a stone to my death, to recognise the irrevocability of my futile existence.

Peace, eternal peace after the infernal rattle of guns and the screaming of the engine...

I felt nothing of this.

A unique masterpiece from the bright-coloured brush of the Creator, the earth drew nearer, brilliant and gleaming in the life-giving midday sun.

I had closed my eyes and was hanging unconscious in my straps...

A sound of bells rose into the air. Their tones rang bright and clear over the martyred, battered earth. Calves gambolled boisterously over the Normandy meadows... the gentle lowing of the cows.

Deathly weary, I opened my eyes and automatically braced my legs. They were caught in a hedge, my head banged against a wooden garden fence and I sank into a dreamless oblivion.

⋆ ⋆ ⋆

Some Normandy peasants had watched my fall. They ran up quickly and extricated me from my harness. While their neighbouring village was being consumed by a sea of flames, all that was left of the crashing aircraft, they carried my unconscious form to a nearby farm.

I was alive but I did not regain consciousness for many hours. I was lying in a huge peasant bed. A thick, quilted eiderdown drove the sweat out of all my pores. Around me stood men eager to help, staring at me with compassion. An old bent peasant held a glass of pale yellow liquid in his trembling hands. "*Pauvre ami, vòilà un cidre...*"

With a feverish hand I took the glass and eagerly drank the bitter apple spirit.

I looked gratefully at the people round the bed. By rights they should have hated the Germans who had unleashed the fury of war that was now burning, scarring and murdering their Normandy, destroying their country...

Here on the edge of war the true nature of humanity was to be found – the all-understanding and forgiving readiness to come to the help of humanity. And while a girl wiped my hot brow with wet towels and stroked my torn hands tenderly, the door was suddenly pushed open violently and two SS men with pointed Tommy-guns burst into the room. The women screamed and to the SS men's "Hands up" replied with a weak "*Nix Anglais*."

I raised my wounded arm. "You can speak German, you know. Just tell me where I am and get hold of a car to take me to Paris."

⋆ ⋆ ⋆

Contusions, torn muscles and slight concussion of the brain. I had flown my last mission over the invasion front.

I was given a private ward in Clichy so that I could have perfect quiet, but there were too many wounded so I asked to be taken among my comrades who had been lying in a Luftwaffe casualty station for a fortnight with serious burns. I found there *Leutnant* Kurt Knebe, the quiet friendly peasant lad from West Pomerania, and *Oberfeldwebel* Knell. They did not disturb me, for they could hardly speak. Their heads were swathed in bismuth bandages and only their eyes, noses and mouths could be seen through small holes.

This mask was an indescribable torture.

Fiery burning and itching, hot sweat and stinking pus... Their food was conveyed to them through a glass tube. Dr Manz had been at this hospital for some days and recognised me. Thus the wheel had come full circle; I was only a spoke in this wheel, thrust and driven willy-nilly by the blind whims of destiny along a pre-ordained path...

⋆ ⋆ ⋆

"So you had another bad night, *Herr Oberleutnant*?"

The pretty young Sister smiled anxiously at me as she arranged my bed.

"Did I? I can't remember anything."

"That's a good thing, then. You must take it very quietly and peacefully if you ever want to become a fighter pilot again."

Angela always found something charming to say. She was adored like an angel in Clichy on account of the peace and serenity that seemed to flow from her. Her real name was Kathe, but someone considered that Angela was better suited to her and so she was known as Angela throughout the whole hospital.

Her laughter was like music and when her hand touched the most painful parts of a wounded man's body it was as soft as a caress. Angela was loved by everyone – not in the coarse sense of possessive love but with the tender protective love suited to an angelic young girl.

"Your masks are coming off today, *messieurs*," she said, as she busied herself with our morning toilet. "I can hardly wait to see the unmasking. You need not be so afraid. Burns are not the worst thing that could have happened. You will still be able to kiss the girls."

"Kiss the girls? I'd rather have a skat board, Angela. Fighter pilots can't live without skat," Knebe mumbled from behind his mask. One could sense the smile and the wrinkles round his eyes beneath the stiff dirty grey lint.

"No, no. I don't believe you. I'd better tell you a fairy story. That fellow over there needn't get so excited... As a poor innocent girl I once heard there was plenty of talk of girls during a game of skat."

"It wouldn't be a bad thing, Sister... you might tell them Hans Andersen's story of the flying coffer." I grew serious. "You see," I said, "we can't get away from flying and it would be wonderful if one could go in a flying coffer to fairyland where there is no war."

Even the serene Angela fell silent. The position to the west of Paris had obviously now become serious and it seemed as though...

Knell interrupted. "What were you doing last night with a Macchi, *Herr Oberleutnant*?"

"A Macchi?"

"You kept screaming that I wasn't firing and finally the night Sister came in."

"If I was raving about a Macchi it must have had something to do with Munchendorf, where I once flew that Italian fighter. We had fetched a Macchi 200 from the Adriatic... from Gorizia... If I were to tell you about it, it would sound like a fairy tale."

"Well, this is the time for fairy tales," said Sister Angela. "Tell us about it, but don't excite yourself."

"Nonsense. We're not kids. I'm sorry, Angela. I didn't mean you. Your stay here must have killed any vestige of the flapper in you. Am I right?"

"You certainly are," she said, with a smile, stripping off Knell's counterpane to make him comfortable.

I began my story.

"Well, to make it brief, on take-off, when I was about 150 feet up and adjusting the propeller – the Macchi 200 had an adjustable propeller for take-off and normal flight – the motor conked. I'd got enough height, but when the whole length of Munchendorf lies in front of you it gives you rather a shock. You have to do the unpardonable and turn back. So I banked to put her down again on the airfield – the famous death bank which every pupil is taught to avoid like the plague from his very first flying lesson.

"With the greatest difficulty I got round with the nose well down until I was now only thirty feet up and then the accident happened. A hut stood in my way and I had no alternative but to go straight through it. Yes, right through the middle of the roof. On the other side, the steel mast of a high-tension circuit took a good third of my right wing off. The controls had gone west and the rudder was broken. I could just operate the stick although it was very heavy, but there was definitely no response from the rudder. The Macchi bounced from the mast into the air and the moment came when my life loomed up before me as it does before a doomed man. You've all experienced that. The next moment the aircraft stalled, the nose whipped down with its heavy engine and the Macchi dropped like a dead leaf into a vineyard.

"And then came the fairy tale. I was sitting well strapped into my seat with everything breaking up around me. Unwittingly I had switched off and applied the emergency brakes.

"In a flash I was hurled twenty yards away from the Macchi. It happened so quickly that I didn't realise it. That was the 20th April 1942 and I shall never forget that date. That evening I had to treat the whole *Staffel*; it was a real pilot's beanfeast."

"I've done the same thing, *Herr Oberleutnant*," said Knell, breaking the ensuing silence. "I once crashed an Me 109 from 12,000 feet and couldn't release the hood. I worked like a madman in the spinning machine. I had unstrapped my belt and was pushing with all my weight against the cabin roof. Then the flying speed made me jump from my seat and, half crazy with fear, I beat my fists on the perspex till they bled. No use. And then I grew calm and resigned myself to my fate, and, as you said, *Herr Oberleutnant*, the film of my life passed before my eyes.

"Suddenly I found myself hanging on my parachute barely 300 feet above the ground. There had been a tremendous jolt on my back.

"But how I got out I shall never know. From the colossal strain of a spin from 12,000 feet the Messerschmitt must have been torn apart and this was what had saved me at the very last second.

"After that I'd had enough of the 'flying coffin' and I applied for transfer to an Fw 190 go group."

Angela jumped up quickly. "You're making me forget all the others. But next time I shall tell the stories; they won't be so exciting but they'll be far better for my patients."

⋆ ⋆ ⋆

Three days later all of us were back at Villacoublay.

The position had become so critical that no one wanted to remain in Clichy for the Americans to capture the hospital. We felt more comfortable back with the *Staffel*.

Preparations were in progress for a hasty retreat. Boxes and trunks were packed and loaded on to lorries. No one knew that a huge stock of brandy, Cointreau and Benedictine remained in the cellar. Anything that could not be drunk must be destroyed according to orders. Hundreds of yards away from the castle a magnificent intoxicating aroma filled the air.

Any machines that could not be flown had to be scuttled. In sections the pathetic remains of the once so proud "*Grünherz*" *Gruppe* made its way eastward.

This was the balance sheet on the 19th August 1944. Out of the eighty pilots in action at the beginning of the invasion only six remained fit for flying. These figures did not take into account the reinforcements which were in the neighbourhood of 100 per cent dead or wounded within a few days of their transfer.

Who would not have been critical about the organisation of the German fighter arm? We had all flown in vain.

⋆ ⋆ ⋆

A lorry brought the wounded pilots slowly home.

Collapse... The endless stream of fighter-bombers mercilessly attacked the retreating columns. A wild urge for self-preservation reigned on these retreat roads. Every man for himself...

Defeated, desperate troops on foot, on bicycles, in clumsy peasant waggons and motor vehicles... On all the roads leading eastwards from Paris waited despairing girls, the German news service and staff employees. Their organisation had been scattered to the wind lik chaff; their leaders had left and they waited in the ditches with little chance of being transported home.

"Take us along with you, boys..."

Looking for protection and shivering with cold they crawled in among the wounded.

A proud army – for years feared for its steel strength and invincibility, fled along the bombed roads and through the shotup villages of France towards the German frontier. Civilians, cursing and delighted at their defeat, shot at them as they retreated.

Chapter Nine

THE improbable had become fact. After the breakthrough, despite confused and unobtrusive rearguard actions, the French front now lay on the German frontier.

With the greatest possible speed the last reserves were flung into new positions and then – what no military expert in the whole world would have believed possible – the allied troops broke through the west-wall fortifications and the Maginot line.

Everyone in Germany, however, knew that the war was drawing relentlessly to a close and that it would have to end with a German collapse unless a miracle happened.

This miracle was awaited passionately. The first secret weapons appeared at the front. And even though with simple soldier humour the men chalked up in their dug-outs slogans such as: "*Wir alten Affen sind die deutschen Wunderwaffen*!" and "God Bless the PBI" each of them hoped that the promises given by the High Command would be fulfilled. Some powerful antidote against the Damocles sword, some desperate remedy against collapse...

If everything had been in vain why should we have endured this infernal martyrdom for years on end, why had so much blood and human life been sacrificed? Millions of dead men mouldered forgotten in their graves and their death had been useless, meaningless. It could not be so! It must not be so!

Thus the troops consoled themselves with the daily reiterated promises of new reinforcements, of new devastating, decisive weapons.

Was there anything behind it or was it only hot air?

Tank-busters were delivered to the army and anyone who saw their effect when used against the overwhelming enemy tank attacks could have been convinced of the vast superiority of the German weapons. To counter the Asdics which had caused such havoc among the German U-boats, the navy was now equipped with schnorkel-carrying submarines. The Luftwaffe would regain superiority in the air over Germany now that turbojets and rocket planes were being mass-produced.

New V-weapons were due to appear any day now and, even if the V-1 had lost its terror for the enemy, its far more powerful successors would effectively destroy England's war-industry centres. Rumours passed from mouth to mouth. The day was not far distant when New York would be bombarded by rockets fired from Germany!

Despite the devastating defeats, the strangling pincer hold on the East and West Fronts, despite the daily increasing destruction of the war industries by massed bombing attacks which ravaged and burnt deeper and deeper into the homeland; despite all these obvious proofs of his own impotence the German soldier still believed in the decisive victory-bringing miracle.

* * *

"*Servus*, Heilmann. Glad to have you back with us."

It was a pleasant reunion. The *Kommandeur* hastily pushed a file of papers for signature to the edge of his big writing desk. He stood up quickly and stretched out both hands to the new arrival.

"Now sit down. Let's see how you look. Are you fit again?"

"I hope so. Otherwise I'd have stayed at home. It wasn't a pleasant leave-taking this time in this tricky situation."

"I know. There must have been a lot of tears. The Rhine's now become a battlefield."

"Not so much that," I said, "but..."

"Hello! What a sight for sore eyes." Neumann had come in, unobserved. "You must excuse me, sir, but no one answered my knock. I need those papers urgently about the test flights." The Adjutant fumbled nervously in the file. "Yes, this is it, but you haven't signed it yet."

Choosing a pen from the inkstand and handing it to the *Kommandeur*, he nodded with a smile at me. "It was high time you turned up. You'll have a fit when you see what they're sending us now in the way of new blood. They only last a few days here and there..."

Neumann hastily grabbed the papers which had now been signed and hurried from the room.

What an odd fellow, I thought. Adjutants seem to be the same all the world over. However much time they've got, they worry themselves sick, and whenever they get an ordinary sheet of foolscap in their hands they have to make out that they're as busy as hell.

"Yes, Neumann's right. The good old days of Oldenburg are numbered, but I don't mind telling you that we've got a far better 'crate'coming."

"A jet?"

"Not yet, but a new Focke. The 'Strangler' has been improved and becomes the Dora 9. I'm very pleased with it. Twenty to thirty miles an hour faster and a methane supercharger in case of trouble. Can be flown for half an hour and gives an additional twenty miles an hour. This morning I spotted a reconnoitring Spitfire at 2,400 feet south of Bremen. You should have seen the bloody circus. Now we're faster than the chaps over there. I can tell you, it's a wonderful feeling."

"You're telling me. And what about the Spitfire, did you shoot it down?"

"How can you ask such a thing?"

"Congratulations."

"Thanks, Heilmann. Help yourself... Cigars, cigarettes, whatever you want. I've got another few minutes' work here and then we'll go over to the hangar."

I snipped the end off a Havana cigar and went over to the wall on which a 6-foot map was nailed.

Hmm... it did not look very promising... The breakthrough region which the allies would attempt seemed to lie between Trier and Aachen. Canadians and British in the north on the left wing, just as in the invasion. Holland had been to a great extent flooded. In this way the front had been shortened considerably.

"Well, Heilmann, I'm ready. Let's go."

Weiss grabbed his flying helmet. "Have you ever seen one of our new kites ?"

"No. I wanted to see the 'Raven' again first," I said with a smile, joking on the code name which the *Kommandeur* had borne on the invasion front.

There was a lively exchange of conversation as we made our way across the airfield. After having been almost seven weeks away after my concussion I thought that I had entered a completely new world. It was full of strange pilots. Only among the ground staff did I recognise old and trusted faces.

We stood in silence for a moment examining the new Focke.

Good God! She's undergone a bit of a change The old potbellied gentleman has become a slender pretty lady with the exciting name of Dora 9... I find her a bit too long in the leg.

"But inside she's like the old Focke," I said with a look of surprise. "Only the old radial engine's gone and it's now fitted with an in-line Jumo 213 from the Junkers motor works."

We examined the new fighter from every angle.

"What kind of prop is that, then?"

"The blades are broader and it gives a far better drive. You should just see how you're glued to your seat when you take off."

"What's she like on turns?" I asked thoughtfully, tapping the new auxiliary fin in front of the tail unit which gave the machine the necessary stability. The Dora 9 was nearly five feet longer than its elder brother.

"Oh, I'm quite pleased with her. She's not a bad bus. Has to look like that. Greater speed and a longer body must logically give a greater turning radius. Keeps her steadier in a split-arse turn. Zoom and flatten out."

"*Jawohl, Herr Hauptmann*!" I clicked my heels and put two fingers to my cap with a smile. "Shall we take her up for a flip?"

"Splendid idea. Why not? We've never yet had a mock combat."

Half an hour later the whole *Staffel* on the field was looking spellbound at the breath-taking game being played between two slim silver aircraft, making patterns with their vapour trails against the blue sky. With daring stunts – climbing turns, mad dives nearly to the ground and break-neck zooms, elegant loops, corkscrew rolls and steep stalling turns – the *Gruppen Kommandeur* and his senior *Staffelkaptän* were trying out the new anti-tank fighter.

The joy of flying...

The age-old dream and the eternally youthful aspiration of all youngsters. To be as free as a bird... Above, the glorious freedom of the air, and below, the bright-coloured relief of the abandoned earth. Smooth, blue-green patches of water, broad mountain peaks with their chasms, slippery glaciers and sparkling snow peaks. And in between, the gay mosaic of cultivated fields; the green, yellow and red patchwork of the fields... The red tints of village roofs and the misty haze over the industrial cities...

Taking off from Biarritz, I had once been able to enjoy this pilot's existence to the full. At 36,000 feet, I left the Atlantic Ocean, with the Bay of Biscay behind me; the wild mighty range of the Pyrenees stretched in long, drawn-out, clean-cut crests to the Alps, whose glaciers glittered in eternal snow and ice with all the colours of the rainbow. On my right, as far as the eye could see, a carpet of gleaming blue, the Mediterranean...

No earth-bound man can ever understand the pilot when he tries to find words to express this intoxicating and beautiful dream. Whoever has practised the art of flying, sporting like a gigantic bird through the air, has left all the cares and burdens of this world far behind him. The serene joyous freedom, the untrammelled liberty which we, who live on the ground, have to renounce, make the pilot a new man, and more than this – the aircraft obediently follows the slightest pressure on the controls until, welded to its pilot, it too becomes a new being!

Pilots often speak with enthusiasm of this experience, the eternal hunger for the sky and the clouds, and they always add plaintively: "If only they wouldn't throw great chunks of iron at you!" And the pilot is invariably right. Weapons of the murder trade are utterly unsuited to this youthful dream of intoxicating beauty.

⋆ ⋆ ⋆

Professor Tank, the designer of the Focke-Wulf 190, had arrived. He wanted to talk to the men who would soon be flying the new aircraft against the enemy. The peat fire crackled gently on the hearth and spread its characteristic odour through the room. It was a picturesque sight, this sooty, red-tiled hearth with the glowing lumps of peat, but it gave little heat and the few men sitting there in the twilight of a September evening had drawn their chairs closer to the fire. The group consisted of only a few officers, for such a conference had to be kept secret – the *Gruppe Kommandeur*, four *Staffelkapitaen*, the Adjutant, a technical officer and the professor.

So this was Germany's greatest genius among aircraft designers!

At first sight he looked sympathetic, a fair-sized, strong, broad-shouldered type. Nothing flabby about his face. Energetic and resolute... Nothing of the professor about him as one usually finds in these famous bald-headed men. By nature, too, he was natural, young and full of vitality.

The pilots warmed to him at once and we were soon in the middle of an animated conversation. We learned that the Fw I90, or Dora 9, was only a temporary urgently-needed solution, mainly because the Junkers engine works had in their yards enormous quantities of this Jumo 213, which had been built to satisfy the demands of the German operational machines which were now out of the question.

Tank's aim was the Ta 142 – a high-altitude fighter with a ceiling of 42,000 feet. Pressurized cabin... Naturally the best engined aircraft in the world. It was practically ready for mass production.

His claim did not seem so natural to his experienced listeners, and Weiss said: "Provided the others don't go to sleep in the meantime, *Herr* Professor."

Tank seemed a little depressed that anyone should doubt the merits of his design. And then those of his audience who had the gumption to read between the lines learned that the competitive struggle between the German aircraft designers was endangering the conduct of the war. Tank, of course, did not have to bother about these intrigues because he was well appreciated – and that only thanks to Hitler's backing had Willi Messerschmitt been in a position to put his Me 109 into mass production, although completely redesigned as everyone here knew. The Me 109 was, in its time, the best fighter plane in the world, vastly superior to the normal two and one-and-a-half deckers, but... it had had its day!

Now it had been over-designed, and deteriorated with every alteration. In the narrow fuselage there was no longer any more room for the traditional equipment rendered imperative by improvements in the enemy machines, such as additional armament and superchargers. Holes were cut in the sides and the projecting parts covered with streamlined plates. On its first appearance this once outstanding aircraft was nicknamed "The Bulge".

"But why do they go on building her when the Focke is a far better machine?" This was the question the pilots invariably asked when the Me 109 was mentioned.

The jet fighters, the Arado and the Me 262, were criticised. The Me 163, the "Comet", had to prove itself before it won any laurels.

"And how goes it with the output? In other words, what's left over after the four-engined bombers?" asked one of the *Staffelkapitaen*.

"If only your *General* Galland could conjure up as many pilots as we could produce machines! Don't laugh, gentlemen. I'm not telling you any lies when I assure you that at the moment 4,000 machines a month are being turned out. Within four months at the latest we shall have reached the Anglo-American armament potential. Speer is behind this drive like the devil pitch-forking lost souls..."

"Well, if in four months we haven't been knocked out of the sky..." Weiss's words rang out harsh and clear – words which echoed through the room like a cry of warning... And when the technical officer asked what was the present estimated figure of American aircraft production per month, Professor Tank had no answer to give.

On the 3rd October I wrote pointedly in my diary: "Castles in Spain or facts? Self-deception or conviction? Despite his great charm and his obvious technical knowledge I could not help feeling that everyone at the top is working for his own pocket, including Professor Tank."

And yet, as God knows, there is more at stake than that.

★ ★ ★

As a last unexpected surprise the pilots of the "*Grünherz*" *Gruppe* were sent to Oldenburg and the time sped by as on a pleasant leave. Theatres, cinemas, hotels with comfortable lounges for gossip.... In the actual training station there was a special cinema for the permanent staff. Alternate variety shows and dances arranged by the different *Staffeln* stationed in the nearby villages – the pilots in private billets – engendered a carefree optimism.

Day after day the new Fockes were flown in mock air battles, and the workshops were given the necessary expert technical instruction.

The "*Grünherz*" *Gruppe* was re-equipped and was ready for action again. The new pilots could not be termed reinforcements in the ordinary sense, for most of them were experienced fliers from disbanded bomber *Staffeln*. This caused great difficulties to some of the pilots when it came to keeping their place in the air circus. The bombers knew nothing of aerobatics. The fighter pilots called their blind-flying comrades "Air Cabbies" – and the manoeuvring of the fast single-seaters proved far more difficult than one would have believed at the start.

Each *Staffel* had two or three flying officers and twenty *Gefreiter* or *Feldwebel* pilots. With the exception of our commander, Hans Dortenmann, who had been promoted to *Gruppen Kommandeur*, and myself, all the other flying officers were strangers. The non-commissioned pilots included Patt, Knell, Gusser the Tyrolean, and von der Jechten. *Jagdgeschwader* 26 had produced *Leutnant*s Prager and Cromm so that our *Gruppe* could put into the air enough officers with fighter experience.

The rearmament included a fixed adjustment[1] of the guns on a point about 120 yards ahead of the machine. There was target practice so that we could try out the new weapons, above all a 2-cm. quick-firing cannon synchronised to fire through the propeller blades.

The III./*Jagdgeschwader* 54 was once more ready for action.

[1] This focusing all weapons on a fixed point 120 yards ahead of the aircraft meant that, if the target was further off, the piot had to aim several notches higher in his sights, and lower when the angle was less.

Chapter Ten

SUPERIOR weapons always decide the outcome of the battle. But they must be put into the battle at its peak and anyone who does not observe this military truism lets victory slip through his fingers.

On Hitler's orders the Arado and the Me 262 – the first jet fighter in the world with a speed of over 600 miles an hour – went into action as bombers. A crazy asinine obstinacy insisted that bombs must be dropped on London and these valuable, irreplaceable machines carried a thousand pounds of bombs to southern England – a single thousand-pound bomb! And a single Boeing replied with twenty times that amount of explosive.

A sullen murmur of rage ran through the ranks of the fighter pilots. Was the High Command so absolutely devoid of sense that it could no longer see that the jet fighter, with its superior speed and heavy fire power, was the only possible salvation against destruction from the devastating rain of bombs? In the case of a defensive attack which had become almost futile in the face of enemy air cover, the 200-mile-an hour faster jet fighters could seek out their targets when and where they pleased.

The Boeing and Liberator staffels would be powerless against the wicked fire of four 2-cm quick-firing cannon. Their silhouettes appeared like barn doors in the sights and it was impossible to miss one of these giant "crates".

But suggestions of the most urgent nature were pointless. It was like talking to a stone wall. London must be razed to dust even if the whole of Germany became a pile of rubble in the attempt!

The General of the Fighters, on his own responsibility, therefore stuck out his own neck when he commissioned *Major* Nowotny to form a special *Kommando Gruppe*. From the Hesepe and Achmer airfields on either side of the Mitteland Canal, some ten miles north of Osnabruck, thirty chosen pilots flew the Me 262 trying to show by their number of victories, firstly, that a jet fighter with a thousand-pound bomb was a military folly and, secondly, that the arrow-swift jet fighter represented the future of the flying arm.

The only vulnerable points of the "Turbos", as the fighter pilots christened the Me 262s, were take-off and landing. In spite of starting aids – three rockets below each wing – they got off the ground too slowly. As a result of the enormous demands on the material from dangerously high temperatures, the starting of the two turbines could only be speeded up in easy stages. As opposed to piston-engined aircraft in which the throttle is pushed well home on take-off, the pilot of a jet machine had to manoeuvre his fuel throttle slowly and gently. At this moment both the rev counters must be watched and the pilot had to concentrate on them while his machine was taking off.

Those were long terrifying minutes during which any enemy fighter diving out of the clouds could bring inevitable death. The same thing applied to landing. Thus Fockes had to throw a protective net over the airfield until the "Turbos" were well under way.

With this end in view Dortenmann and I flew southwards with our staffels on October 2th and landed at Achmer and Hesepe respectively.

The good old days of Oldenburg were over.

Now things were really cooking. The new Fockes must show their superiority at any moment. Each day brought another mass-bombing attack by four-engined bombers and swarms of Mustangs and Thunderbolts always escorted them.

At the outset the Dora 9 was not always recognised by the Yanks. It bore a certain resemblance to the Mustang and, while our own flak opened fire immediately on us as enemy machines, the Thunderbolt pilots often thought that they had their own comrades ahead of them. This soon changed and they learned very quickly on the other side what kind of tough eggs the two airfields on the Mitteland Canal had hatched.

And while they were busy in the air keeping a good distance from the "Turbos" they hung like thick bunches of grapes over the two airfields watching the ticklish moment of take-off and landing.

Again and again a handful of brave Focke pilots waded into the enemy swarms and provided an effective air umbrella for the turbos. Nevertheless despite our superior machines we suffered great losses and after two days Dortenmann, who was based at Achmer, had to ask for reinforcements. I was forced to do the same.

⋆ ⋆ ⋆

Staffel 9 had made its headquarters about three miles from the airfield – a peaceful, idyllic village at the fringe of the war. If the absence of their sons fighting in the front line did not interfere too much with their work in the fields, the Malgarten peasants would be able to last out the war for a long time yet.

The country round Bramsche is very rich. Generations of hard-working hands have carved out for themselves a comfortable existence and pride of property gleams in the weatherbeaten eyes of the Westphalians.

In every tavern countless sides of bacon and sausages hung from the massive, sooty oak beams. Shaking his head, some infantryman would count as many as five or six hams; but, since a pig is known to run around on four legs before it is slaughtered, a lot more must be hanging up there.... It was no wonder that this was the greatest pork-producing region in Europe and there was no peasant house in which one would not find a nice slice of sucking pig.

For the staffel Malgarten was a paradise, a Garden of Eden. Sucking pig, goose, ham, sausages and pork... It was really too much to expect in the sixth year of the war.

The hungry ground staff began to look like well-fed hounds and many of the older *Gefreiter*s had to order a new pair of trousers, for so much consumption of pork had made it impossible to button up the original pair.

The fat postman cursed the sudden flood of parcels and packages which suddenly flowed into his office after long years of peaceful service. Samples from this paradise were sent to all parts of Germany.

* * *

"Shouldn't we go to church today?" said Patt, making his favourite joke. "A soldier has a right to do that, *Herr Oberleutnant*."

"You're quite in order, Patt. Go by all means if you like."

"Oh no. All of us must go. What do you say if we give the old Bramsche folk a treat and let them see us goose-stepping up to the altar? Normally they only see us from a distance and they're angry because we've grabbed the best places in their barns! Hee! hee! hee!"

"Patt's right, *Herr Oberleutnant*. If we put in an appearance once in the church we shall have won the day. I know that from the *Stabsfeldwebel*."

Everybody waited eagerly for what *Leutnant* Barten-Foss would now produce by way of a horror story. "I think he wants a bit of encouragement."

"I suppose you mean he wants a new photo for his notecase? Hee! hee! hee! " croaked Patt spreading the last of the butter on a thick slice of white bread. Everybody laughed, for they all knew the *Stabsfeldwebel*'s pastime.

"Yes. Go on, Barten," I said, with interest.

"The *Stabsfeldwebel*'s having a lot of difficulty with the inn-keeper's daughter. His latest girl friend insists that he has to play the grand seigneur in Papa's parlour if she's going to flutter her eyelids at him. But it's no good. He can't get upstairs to the bedroom in spite of all his wiles. Then he got a brilliant idea. He must go to church. Love in these villages is so very..."

"The *Stabsfeldwebel* going to church. What a wonderful idea," said Knell, roaring with laughter.

"You can laugh, Knell, for now he's stormed the citadel and won himself a bride."

A roar of laughter ran round the table.

The orderly switched off the wall-bracket lights. The sun shone red over the tops of the pines and through the open windows could be heard the sound of church bells. Yes, it was Sunday.

At the briefing on the previous evening the *Major* had promised the Focke pilots their Sunday rest. They should hold themselves ready for a late mission after four o'clock. He would give them plenty of warning.

So the staffel took plenty of time that day over breakfast. Usually it was swallowed down in haste and it was still dark when I set out in my Citroen for Hesepe.

As I got up from the table the others were sitting cornfortably in a corner for their after-breakfast cigar. Skat and chess boards, newspapers and magazines lay on the table. There was no cause for boredom.

It looked like being a fine autumn day.

"If any of you has anything on I suggest he gets it finished by three o'clock this afternoon."

"My dear Willi, can you explain to me what the hell there is to do in this negro kraal except play skat and eat?" said Knebe with a laugh. He had been back three days with the *Staffel*. His burns had healed surprisingly well and only the smooth red scars round his wrists were visible.

"Actually I wanted to drive to Osnabruck. I put it off yesterday afternoon because there was a Thunderbolt attack and I suddenly saw below us those pathetic ruins. I'll drive through the neighbourhood... Perhaps I shall find some nice country inn or something. I shall be back by midday. Any of you want to come along?" Knebe and Patt, my old pals from the invasion front, accepted and, together with Tunnes, the mess orderly, who had brought a picnic basket, we started off on our proposed trip.

Leaving behind us all the worries of forthcoming missions we drove expectantly in the bright Sunday sunshine....

Small lakes, dark copses nestling between small hillocks; broad sturdy peasant farms, most of them with gigantic thatched roofs.... At the gates like age-old watchmen stood gnarled oaks or mighty limes. Everything was outlined in clear heavy contours. The colours were striking – green, blue and red patches.

It was not surprising when one drove through the country that the inhabitants were so tough, silent and uncompromising.

The four of us had decided to drive to the outskirts of the Teutoburger Wald. From the air the neighbourhood round Ibbenbuhren and Tecklenburg looked particularly pretty.

"It was a good idea of yours, *Herr Oberleutnant*," said Patt cheerfully. I had stuck a cigar into his mouth and Patt swore it was the first time he had smoked anything so magnificent. It was comical to see him put the cigar to his lips with outspread fingers, puffing away peacefully, his stick-out ears moving at each puff above a freckled face.

"You're right, Patt," said Knebe. "The Chief's got the right idea. This eternal skat and rummy playing gets on my nerves and I'm a complete duffer at chess or draughts."

Patt agreed.

Tunnes – a youngster from Cologne who, owing to heart trouble, had become a slow phlegmatic man prone to an occasional hysterical outburst (the *Stabsfeldwebel* could not understand why the *Staffelkapitän* kept this "Weeping Willie") – was enjoying himself quietly in his corner with the basket of ham, eggs and schnapps on his skinny knees. He was thinking that in this way he had escaped from the station messroom where from morning till night he was chiwied and chased by one officer after another, fulfilling all their wishes. None of them realized how badly they treated him. This morning, however, somebody else could do the dirty work, and he smiled to himself like a truant schoolboy.

⋆ ⋆ ⋆

Shortly after we had left, the telephone rang.

The rummy game in the corner continued. At last Max, the orderly, came in from the pantry and took up the receiver.

"One moment, please, *Herr Major*." Then he told thc rummy party that *Major* Nowotny was on the line and wanted to speak to the *Oberleutnant*. *Leutnant* Kolodzie, a small, insignificant pilot, jumped up.

"*Leutnant* Kolodzie here. Yes, sir. No, sir. The *Herr Oberleutnant* has gone out for a drive. Yes, sir... at ten minutes past eight. I'll do that, sir."

He returned with wrinkled brows to the other three. Before he had uttered a word they knew that their Sunday rest was over.

"I think we'd better slip off ourselves. What do you think, Ernst?" asked *Gefreiter* Burt.

"Hmm. I don't know." Kolodzie seemed to be in a flaring rage. He shook his mop of fair hair angrily. "I'm supposed to drive after the staffel commander and get into the air with everything we've got. The *Oberfeldwebel* has already been informed and is getting the 'kites' out."

There were long faces.

A light truck took the pilots out to the airfield. The rummy players, Kolodzie, Burt and *Feldwebel* King and Fuchs, *Leutnant* Barten-Foss and *Feldwebel* Knell, who were in their rooms writing letters, all assembled. Their hearts beat faster when they thought that they had got to set out with only six aircraft.

Kolodzie was a cunning old fox. As a *Gefreiter* he had been in fighters and had been promoted to officer for bravery. He sensed the nervousness of his comrades.

"Don't get in a panic. I'll see to it that we join up with Dortenmann. Let's hope that the Achmer boys haven't taken a powder too."

They were soon at the airfield. Parachutes fastened – they already lay on the wings of the aircraft – and then quickly into the cockpit.

They started their engines at about 8.14. A few minutes later the turbos were taxying onto the runway. Only six aircraft that day.... A screaming wail and they took off, leaving long rocket trails behind the wings. The Fockes needed only half the length of the airfield and usually started from their pens but the concrete runway had had to be lengthened 500 yards for the turbojets.

While *Staffel* 9 with a couple of spotters circled above the airfield, turbo after turbo took off. Nose wheels and undercarriages were retracted and in a wide sweep the six joined the aircraft that had presumably taken off from Achmer. Their target was a bomber stream which at this extraordinarily early hour was attacking central Germany.

Kolodzie was alone. No one had turned up from Achmer. Over the radio the ground control gave orders to remain air borne another quarter of an hour until Dortenmann had taken off to cover the landing of the returning turbos.

"Victor," snapped *Leutnant* Kolodzie.

He looked round contentedly at his pals. Not an enemy fighter in sight. It was quite unnecessary for the *Major* to have ordered them to gain altitude, for it was far too early for the enemy fighters. They were never particularly keen on starting out in the half-light and they would take a good hour to get here.

Below the Fockes gleamed the silver ribbon of the Mitteland Canal which flows westwards at Rheine into the DortmundEms Canal, joining the Elbe and the Ems and at the same time the canal network system in north-west German and Dutch territory. In the blinding early-morning sunshine they recognised the dark chain of the Weser with the deep triangular cut of the Porta Westfalica. To the south the Teutoburger Wald appeared on the horizon.

A glance at his watch. They had to remain in the air another five or six minutes. The six aircraft continued to make wide circles at 6,000 feet.

Then came information from the ground station. Thunderbolts had been spotted – about forty of them – a few minutes before, south of Osnabruck.

Hell, thought Kolodzie. That's too hot for us. He turned off northwards so as to be able to land at Hesepe when their flying time had lapsed.

"Barten to Kolodzie. Attention. Something glittering above us to starboard, right above the sun."

"You're right. It's those bloody Thunderbolts. Don't lose your head. Perhaps they won't see us. We're going down."

Cautiously they turned north-west and got ready to make their run-in. Too late. Like a flash of lightning the heavy yellow-checkered Thunderbolts dived on the six Fockes.

A bitter dog-fight developed in the proportion of about seven to one. The six were broken up immediately and this sealed their fate.

Feldwebel Knell was the only one to take the right action. He yanked his Dora 9 about and streaked away from the diving Americans as fast as he could to the south-east. Utilising the superior speed of his aircraft, he roared over the Teutoburger Wald between the blind clearings away from his four pursuers and landed with his machine badly damaged – the undercarriage would not lower – on Munster-Handorf.

Leutnant Kolodzie flung his machine about the sky trying to shake off his pursuers. In a desperate head-on attack he shot a Thunderbolt down in flames but there were too many hounds after this one poor hare. Kolodzie could not get away and his pursuers stuck grimly on his tail. This veteran fighter pilot who was universally beloved for his great modesty met his fate. His Dora 9 hit the ground near the village of Sudende and exploded.

Fuchs and King stuck together and were able to help each other. When the first jets returned they hurried to their aid. The Thunderbolts broke up in a panic but they did not let their victims out of their sight and when Fuchs and King wanted to fly off and land during a new turbo attack they were hit by incendiary tracers. Both of them crashed a few yards away from each other at Rieste in a wood-encircled field.

Gefreiter Burt met a pilot's death over Malgarten and crashed in flames only a few yards behind the *Staffel* mess.

Leutnant Barten-Foss jumped from his burning machine near the airfield. He banged against the tail unit and broke a leg, but both he and Knell had survived once more.

The dead pilots were buried in Bramsche on the 8th October. They were laid to rest near each other. The morning sun cast its beams over the new graves... just as three days before it had shone through the open window of the mess on the four dead men who still had no idea that their days were already numbered as they sat there happily playing cards.

★ ★ ★

We returned about midday. In splendid fettle the four of us got out of the car; like heedless children the terrible news upset us so much that for the first time in my life I wept tears of rage. In my fury I got back into the car and drove at full speed through the narrow streets of the little town. Pedestrians jumped back onto the pavements cursing me, and tte good folk of Bramsche, disturbed in their Sunday rest, shook their heads with disapproval. At fifty miles an hour the Citroën bumped over the small potholed road that led to the Mitteland Canal. I crossed a stone bridge and turned left. I was livid. Sacrificing my staffel like that... I was already in Achmer.

The airfield and the mess... A scream of brakes and the car pulled up. I was already in the dining-room where some twenty officers were drinking their soup.

"One moment, please, *Herr Major*."

Nowotny looked up in surprise and somewhat disagreeably at this man with the bitter face who had just burst in. He put down his spoon and rose slowly to his feet.

Nowotny took my arm and led me from the room.

"My dear Heilmann, I quite understand you. I know what you want to..."

Funny, I thought. I don't even know what came over me. Yes, now I remember what I wanted to say to Nowotny. I went off calmly with this popular and revered fighter pilot who wore the highest order for bravery, the Oakleaves with Swords and Diamonds of the Knight's Cross. I also admired this slim courageous man from the Ostmark, but now I was in a filthy rage and I exploded.

"Was that absolutely necessary, *Herr Major*? You give us a day off and I drive a few of my pilots out for a peaceful Sunday morning and while I'm away you send six of my 'crates' to their death."

Nowotny turned pale. He pushed me into a leather armchair.

"My dear fellow, I didn't know that it would start so early."

"You're in full command here, *Herr Major*. You don't have to give orders to take off. You don't have to be so keen about a few more aircraft shot down after the smashing success you've had during the past weeks."

"Heilmann, with the best will in the world, I won't put up with any criticism. If you don't pull yourself together I'll have you chucked out."

There was an oppressive silence and we stared at each other. Then the *Major* poured out a brandy, handed it to me, and poured out one for himself. "Look, you may be right, and we must offset your heavy losses against our successes. I won't forget that at the right moment, Heilmann, if I may put the cards on the table. In a fortnight we shall, I hope, be in a position to do so."

"*Herr Major*, I have a request to make."

"Well, go ahead. I'll grant it if it's possible."

"Thank you, sir. My request is that you should spare us for the moment or else our whole *Gruppe* will be liquidated before we can get it going again. The *Gruppen Kommandeur* already moans because we have to hang on the telephone day after day asking for reinforcements."

"What can I do about it, Heilmann? I need air cover over the airfield just as I need air to breathe. Without you the whole of my mission is endangered. So far we've shot down 246 four-engined bombers and a few dozen fighters and you know what our losses are. Three turbos, and one of those was a flying accident and not caused by enemy action."

"I know, *Herr Major*. We have only to obey when you tell us of your successes but we've lost 70 per cent of our men in a week."

"Yes, I see your point. It can't go on like that."

He lit a cigar, apologised and stuck the Havana in my mouth.

"*Herr Major*, I suppose it must be like that. We take off and cover your start, but then you must split up the enemy fighters so that we've got a chance to land and only when our last 'crates' are in their pens should you get going. In the same way, before your turbos land they should remain over the airfield until we've got sufficient altitude. Then the turbos can land."

Nowotny was silent for a long time. He was breathing heavily, and finally he nodded his small head. "It's not a bad idea. You've wasted a good quarter of an hour of my valuable flying time but I don't think it was in vain."

"Thank you, sir. I knew you'd understand."

Chapter Eleven

THE 15th October was a fateful day for the *Staffel*, the blackest day of all, for the same evening another four Fockes were shot down in a bitter dogfight. Two of the boys were killed but the other two managed to crash -land their badly damaged machines in open country and came out unscathed.

The days went by in unrelieved danger.

The losses of the two airfield covering units were slightly less serious. They had collaborated magnificently with the turbos and it was not long before the enemy fighters began to avoid the hornets' nest at Bramsche. Only surprise low-level attacks brought losses in machines and equipment. Several night carpet-bombing raids were unsuccessful.

One day a super-readiness take-off was subjected to one of these low-level attacks. The pilots were already in their machines waiting to take off, but to do so would have been madness. Nevertheless I pushed my throttle full forward and roared off. Eight machines followed me. Hedge-hopping, we sped away to the north and shook off the pursuing Mustangs.

The remaining pilots leaped out of their Fockes and ran for cover. The abandoned machines were naturally an easy target for the Yanks. All of them were shot up.

In the meantime the nine of us who had gained height returned and a wild air battle developed. This time from a superior height with a well-planned attack, my pals and I had a great success. Five Mustangs joined the six burning Fockes round the field and the others fled.

During the ensuing landing Prager spotted a single Thunderbolt which must have lost its formation and was now a straggler. He notified me and while the others landed the two of us set out in pursuit.

The unsuspecting Thunderbolt banked and came into Prager's sights. A hail of bullets tore into its right wing and yet the machine did not burst into flame. The two of us soon noticed that our opponent was an old hand at the game. We had to make it snappy, for the American would obviously call for help and where a single Thunderbolt was to be found the formation could not be far away. So we closed in on him like a pair of pincers and drove him ever lower. A wild chase started at 100 feet above the Mitteland Canal. We continued to register direct hits but these fat-bodied Thunderbolts could take enormous punishment.

The pilot was as brave as a lion. At barely 60 feet he performed a roll, trying to slip away to one side. He then veered off like a hare and left his two pursuers in the blue, but Prager had been following him like a lynx. His tracers pounded relentlessly into the Yankee's fuselage and the Thunderbolt hurtled into a field.

★ ★ ★

Half an hour later Prager and I were already back at Achmer at the scene of our victory. We could follow the trail of the crashed Thunderbolt for more than a hundred yards. Some cows had stampeded in a wild panic but the machine, as it force-landed, had hit and killed two of them. One of them had been in calf and a few yards away from the mother's torn carcase lay the unborn dead calf.

The Thunderbolt was riddled like a colander, but despite this host of direct hits it had not caught fire. It lay there almost undamaged in a green meadow guarded by a soldier from the Pioneer Corps. For the first time after hundreds of dog-fights we had our foe completely intact before our eyes. We climbed into the cockpit and compared the armament and instrument panel with our Focke's. In triumph Prager removed the parachute from the pilot's seat. A small bag containing air-sea rescue equipment was attached to it. So the yellow-checkered "kite" had come from England.

We closely examined this emergency pack; it contained a special cartridge which, on touching the water, automatically inflated a dinghy. A small sail was attached which could also be used as a distress signal. We also found a 'Very' pistol with ammunition, and some small capsules which dissolved in the sea and spread over the surface of the water a brightly-coloured stain, thereby attracting the attention of passing aircraft; there were also concentrated food tablets, a small forced-landing pack worn on the chest and containing a folded silk map of Western Germany, a compass the size of a cuff-link and a small file. Prager picked up his trophies and I could see that the parachute and sail would soon decorate his quarters.

We met the pilot at Achmer. He was an unpleasant-looking immature boy of about twenty with a dirty uniform and unshaven.

Impertinent and cynical, chewing gum between chattering jaws, he gave incomprehensible replies. Obviously he was scared stiff and his saucy manner was an attempt to disguise this fear.

We left the room feeling slightly embarrassed.

"Texas," I muttered, and this word seemed to explain it all.

Generalmajor Galland arrived.

With great excitement he listened to Nowotny's report while his deputy,

Oberst Trautloft, eagerly took down notes.

"My dear Nowotny, I hope you realise that you are my most valuable steed. Without the bare facts which stand in black and white after a week of your reports the jet aircraft will never become a fighter and we shall never be able to reach our goal with it. The most important thing of all is to chase the terror bombers out of the German sky. Only then is there any possibility of producing reliable, mass-produced new weapons which will enable us to bring off a miracle at the last moment."

"I can assure you that whatever lies in my power, *Herr General*, will be done."

"We're all in this bloody mess together if things go badly. Don't let's talk about it any more."

Later the conversation turned on the efforts of the Fighter Staff to create a fighter arm of great striking power with the new types. The German fighter arm had never been stronger numerically but it consisted almost entirely of piston-engined aircraft. That was the burning question.

A handful of idealists had to wage a Sisyphean struggle against know-alls, indolence, treachery and sabotage – and against the wooden-headed planning of the German High Command. The mass-production of turbos had reached a monthly output of a thousand machines. This was Galland's main hope and he was planning to completely re-equip the fighter *Geschwaderen*.

"We shall never get the necessary advantage we need to offset the numerical strength of the enemy in any other way," declared Galland.

Dortenmann and I heaved a sigh of relief. *Oberst* Trautloft assured us that we would be next on the list to be equipped with turbos.

Then the *General* began to speak of the terrible mess-up in the leadership. It was impossible to co-operate with Göring. He groused the whole time about the cowardice of his inefficient fighter *Geschwaderen* and by way of protest had ceased to wear a lot of his medals, including his *Pour le Mérite*.

Dortenmann frowned. We had long since realised that Göring was responsible for our present impotence because instead of building fighters he had wanted to make the West surrender as a result of his bombing.

Today that no longer held good, and Hitler and his paladin would not get it into their heads that the enemy fighter strength, at a most conservative estimate, was 100 per cent greater than the German. And then the cretin kept talking of cowardice. Nothing remained of the *Reichsmarschall*'s former glory and for a long time the fighter pilots had loathed the very sound of his name.

"Yes, and then these fossilised old NSFK[1] *Generals*," Galland went on," particularly Keller. Do you know how he envisages the war in the next few months?"

The audience was all ears.

"You know that the Führer wanted to make the Me 163 *Komet* into a so-called People's Fighter. The *Komet* may be all right and it stood up to its

[1] NSFK was the Nazi Party's own flying organisation – *National-Sozialistische Flieger-Korps*.

tests, but the way the High Command considers it should be used borders on idiocy.

"You know that this rocket fighter is to be shot into the bomber formation at an angle of about 70°. It reaches its ceiling at between 12,000 and 15,000 feet, then the rocket fuel is exhausted. Now it must float down almost like a glider into the enemy's guns. But no laws of aerodynamics will help it to remain airborne. It has to come down as a glider and at best the pilot can bale out. The *Komet* is very cheap to produce, so that in view of its success the aircraft can be sacrificed.

"It's not a bad idea, but now comes the joke. To fly it they need experienced pilots and these little twerps can't see how that can be done.

"But you have piston-engined fighters to fly. You don't need jet aircraft because otherwise 4,000 piston-engined aircraft a month will be wasted.

"And this ridiculous time-saver Keller supports Hitler's plans. He heaps insults on me and my carefully thought out suggestions which are based on true facts and not on wishful thinking; they are turned down time and time again because everybody wants to start winning victories again – if possible tomorrow; certainly in the shortest possible time.

"You don't know what a schemozzle there is in high places. Self-deception, dope and a lot of poppycock talked.

"The Führer was naturally delighted when Keller said grandiosely that he would harness the NSFK to the machine. 'Your People's Fighter, mein Führer, will drive the Anglo-American pest out of the German sky.'

"It takes your breath away, eh? Well, hold tight and listen to this. It's quite simple. Outside each factory, in each city, on various main roads – in short, everywhere – the People's Fighters are already, in their minds, parked like cars. Incidentally, these crackpots have neither built the machines nor got the necessary ground crews to service them, but that's of no account. Let the workers do it themselves. In the early morning before their shift, or in the lunch-break or in the evening before they go to sleep.

"But what I'm going to tell you now beats everything. These are the actual words that were spoken at that crazy session.

"We've been warned. In the NSFK, after intensive training courses, the younger workers are to be transformed into pilots."

"Excuse me interrupting, *Herr General*, but haven't they long since been sent to the front?"

"Let me carry on," said Galland. "I'm only repeating Keller's words. So these workers are to let themselves be catapulted into the sky and save their factories and their country.

"So, my cowardly fighter boys, just have a look how the Fatherland is going to be saved!"

We had not even the courage to laugh; to hear such idiocy, such fantastic ideas of fighter tactics made us shudder. Nowotny said curtly, "We seem to have entered a period of carnival."

Was it any wonder, then, that as a result of such discussion at a high level self-destruction must ensue?

It would not be long before the tireless defender of his plans, this obstinate, ruthless *General* Galland, together with his deputy, *Oberst* Trautloft, and his whole staff, would be kicked out of the Luftwaffe.

In farewell Galland wrote in his war diary:

> *In Germany's darkest moment may God grant strength and faith to the pioneers of a new arm that they may fulfil their task.*
>
> *We must recapture the air supremacy over our country's holy soil and make the German fighter arm the most feared in the world.*
>
> *Adolf Galland,*
> *General of the Fighters*

Chapter Twelve

THE SUCCESS of the turbos exceeded all expectations. The men looked forward hopefully to the day when *Major* Nowotny would hand in the report of their success.

They all wanted to fly these super-machines; thousands of them were hidden in the forests round the Augsburg airfields and yet for some strange reason they were never put into action.

As their success mounted the enemy fighter formations boycotted more and more of the regions round Hesepe and Achmer. Thus the Focke pilots had easier flying conditions and they could bring their new machines into service more successfully. The number of enemy planes shot down increased in both staffel's log books.

The initial mood of depression was transformed into a calm and happy sense of relaxation which could be felt in all the messes.

After a heated quarrel with the station commander, an old dug-out *Oberst* who was still considered capable of fulfilling this duty, I had won my point. The old man could not understand all the requests that the young *Staffelkapitän* put forward for his men. When he refused and there was no other way out, came the famous appeal to the High Command – "I will not tolerate my pilots, between their exhausting operational flights, living in bare holes, while these career soldiers, who know nothing of the war except from the Wehrmacht communiques and from the newspapers, lead a comfortable life in magnificently equipped houses" – and a few days later Hesepe had a new station commander. The newcomer was a cheerful, energetic bomber *Major* called Geissler, who had been grounded from flying on account of having lost a leg.

Major Geissler collected from the divisional officials and bureaucrats, who for years had lived like princes in their new commands, the last chairs, pictures, lamps and curtains of their huts which they had equipped with all the amenities of peacetime and handed them over to the pilots of *Staffel* 9 to brighten up their quarters.

We now sat round the small table in eager, cheerful conversation. I had laid on an official party and invited Dortenmann from Achmer with a few officers from Nowotny's *Gruppe*. *Major* Geissler, the new station commander (whom we wanted to thank), the *Bürgermeister* of Hesepe and his wife, and a few girls from the control-room with whom we were good friends had also been invited. An occasional love affair developed between the pilots and these girls. A splendid show took place while we had our coffee. Among the ground staff there happened to be a magnificent comedian whose eloquence quite bewitched the audience. We had also managed to find a music-hall artiste who earned great applause with his card tricks, juggling and conjuring.

A group of high-ranking officers had gathered round the station commander and the *Bürgermeister* and they were now swapping experiences. *Major* Geissler had a fund of exciting stories to tell of his flights over England. It suddenly turned out that *Leutnant* Prager had been in St Omer when *General* Galland was in command of the Schlageter *Jagdgeschwader* 26. He now told the original story of the shooting down of the English air ace Wing Commander Bader, but he was interrupted half-way through by the comedian, who, now disguised as Quax, the crate-crasher, was attracting everyone's attention. Laughing and smiling, he made his wisecracks about the people present and everything that was known of their private lives. He took the micky out of one pilot because of an unnecessary crash landing. No one knew whether perhaps next spring the stork would not be dropping a baby wrapped up in a bundle down his chimney....

November 5th, 1944

For three weeks now the "*Grünherz*" had been attached to Nowotny's special group.

I had just taken off with my men to cover the landing of the returning turbos which had claimed bomber after bomber from a large formation over Rheine. The staffel was circling at 15,000 feet when the first turbos landed. The ground stations had reported the area free of enemy aircraft. A few Thunderbolts were cruising over Burgsteinfurt, but that was some distance away. The Hesepe turbos had all disappeared from the runway and I made a little detour over Achmer. Losing height slowly, I saw Dortenmann's *Staffel* circling below me.

"Heilmann to Dortenmann. Is everything all right with you?"

"Dortenmann to Heilmann. Two of ours are missing."

The ground station tuned in and ordered me to land. Dortenmann was to remain airborne until the two missing turbos turned up. The Fockes of *Staffel* 9 turned slowly in a broad sweep on to a course of 270°.

I gradually lost height. Below lay Hesepe.

A sudden strange feeling of anxiety caused me to look round. Hell! We seemed to have increased in numbers. Thirty Thunderbolts were coming up behind us. Panic stations. The dozen Fockes followed their leading aircraft which had wrenched itself round and was diving at full speed on the attacking Thunderbolts.

The enemy fire was wildly inaccurate. It is known from experience that it is difficult to aim in a steep dive because the body is wrenched upwards by centrifugal force. The blood streams into the head and for an instant the eyes grow hazy.

I had decided to dive down to Achmer where Dortenmann was still in the air and could wade in to my aid from above.

"Heilmann to Dortenmann. Answer me."

"Victor. What's up?"

"Look out. Gain height. Thirty Thunderbolts on my tail. I'm right above Achmer."

"OK, Willi. Here comes the last turbo. It must be the *Major*."

" Nowotny to Heilmann. Hold it. I'm in the picture."

That was Achmer. I led my *Staffel* to port behind the heavy flak position. The gunners had grasped the situation magnificently and were firing for all they were worth at the diving Thunderbolts. Their concentrated fire must have deafened and blinded the Yanks, for they turned off sharply to starboard.

The next moment Dortenmann dived out of the sun with fourteen machines. Four Thunderbolts crashed in flames at the edge of the airfield. Huge columns of flames rose into the air.

I grabbed my supercharger lever. To our great joy we realised that we could climb faster than the Thunderbolts, which were now also gaining height. (To be above the enemy is half-way to victory.)

This time the Yankees would really get it in the neck.

Dortenmann made off southwards preparatory to a second attack. A turbo sped like an arrow through the Thunderbolt formation. Another of the pot-bellied crates spun to earth. Dortenmann was firing his tracers and two more machines were set on fire.

The Americans never managed to get into their usual circling battle position. They had to watch their opponents who were attacking from all sides. I was in the lead and my staffel had now gained sufficient height above the enemy. The Thunderbolts nervously closed in but they were disorganised. A good defence circle was their only salvation or a close and bitter life-and-death struggle in tight turns such as the German fighters always had to wage against a superior enemy.

Tally-ho! Three Thunderbolts spun down to the deck...

A wild mood of victory obsessed the Focke pilots. They chattered gaily to each other over the intercom. Here was a magnificent revenge for the 5th October. Not one of the Thunderbolts must be allowed to get away.

Nowotny passed like a streak of lightning; four 20mm. quickfiring cannon wreaked death and destruction among the enemy formation. It was pointless starting a fight with such a machine, for it simply outstripped them and caught up with them again exactly as it pleased. It was like an express passing a linesman on the track... and, just as the man would jump aside, the piston-engined fighters had only one chance of escape – to break off and run for it.

Nowotny came on the air. He was out of gas. For safety's sake he would land at Hesepe.

I immediately flew with four machines to take his place on guard. Consequently I had to leave the battle. Dortenmann would be able to cope with the remainder of the Thunderbolts. Pity. Some of them would get away, but Nowotny was more important.

The Fockes followed the turbo as fast as their superchargers would allow.

I could see the *Major*'s aircraft making wide circles preparatory to landing on Hesepe.

At the same moment my heart nearly stopped beating...

A wild hornet drove of about thirty Thunderbolts – probably summoned by their mates to their aid during the battle – dived on Nowotny's turbo.

The *Major* must have spotted the danger at the last second. He tried to take avoiding action but his speed was too slow now that he was coming in to land. Why didn't he bale out?

"Jump, *Major*."

Too late. Hit by devastating bursts from a dozen Thunderbolts, the turbo rolled over on its right wing, blazing furiously.

It crashed behind Malgarten. The explosion blew it to pieces and a column of flames 50 feet high rose for a few seconds in the air until a black cloud of smoke formed, spiralling higher and higher into the blue sky like a fleeing ghost.

Brave *Major* Nowotny was dead.

When the distressed search troops arrived on the scene of the crash they found among the smoking debris only his right hand and the broken oak leaves with the swords and diamonds. The artificial stones had been wrenched from their settings...

Achmer and Hesepe lay under the shadow of deep depression. What a terrible end for an ace like Nowotny. Shot down like a sitting duck without being able to fight. Unconquered and shot down by the pack at the moment of landing... thus died the man who should have proved once and for all the long-awaited and decisive superiority of the jet fighter. Apart from the fact that Nowotny's premature death revealed the fighter *General*'s secret trump card and took the wind out of his sails, the backbone of this special group was now broken.

Despite the posthumously reported success and the sacrifice of one of the best fighter pilots in the world, the ardently desired re-equipment of the fighter groups with jets never matured.

Chapter Thirteen

DECEMBER 16th of this disastrous war year 1944 dawned. A hurricane of fire ruthlessly smashed the enemy's positions. After hours of non-stop bombardments the wall of flame lifted and from the Eifel and the Hoher Venn strong attacking armies left their positions. A stream of tanks broke through the enemy lines. German "King Tigers" flaunted their superiority, destroying all before them, smashing the motorised infantry and forcing them to retreat far back along the front.

The break-through succeeded and, as in the early days of the war, the German High Command planned to advance via Liege and Brussels to the Channel and surround the enemy's armour in a deadly pincer movement.

This unexpected, rapid initial success roused great hopes; the leading tanks stood at the gates of Brussels. Another big hammer-thrust had split the Ardennes front wide open and only with the utmost efforts – by ruthlessly throwing in his last reserves and drawing troops from other fronts – did Eisenhower succeed in stopping the gap and halting the German advance. Enormous formations from the RAF and the US Air Forces flew non-stop over the German advanced units. Marauders appeared like flying infantry; armed with twelve machine-guns, they dived on the attackers. Carpet bombing unceasingly found the target. Typhoons, which had long been discarded as fighters, were brought back into service and with their single weapon – a tank buster – destroyed Tiger after Tiger.

And where was the German Luftwaffe?

It was still resting...

And being equipped...

And waiting for orders...

"What a proper mess-up!"

"You've said it, *Major*. The poor so-and-so's have outwinded themselves. That little sprint as far as Brussels doesn't mean a thing."

Major Geissler and I were standing in front of the large map that hung in the briefing-room. For three days the little blue flags had hardly been moved westwards and there was no need to use the blue pencil any more for changes in the front line.

A strong, almost successful break-through attack had been brought to a standstill.

"I don't know what they're thinking about up top," I said, shaking my head thoughtfully. "That was the very last chance, the last possible well-organised and well-prepared counter-offensive, and they did it without even using the Luftwaffe."

"Hermann wants to wage his own war and didn't intend to gamble his newly-armed Luftwaffe on Rundstedt's account. And yet the risk was worth taking."

"Of course he ought to have taken it. There's absolutely no excuse for him."

"You're right, Heilmann. When you think of the tank commanders there in the front line, when one after another of their magnificent Tigers has to bite the dust without a German fighter making an attempt to knock those lame old Typhoons out of the sky, it hardly bears thinking about."

" I'm not so crazy that I'd gamble my aircraft and my men's lives, but in my opinion it was our duty to help the army. At least we should have made an attempt and shown them on the other side that we're still in the picture." I turned away abruptly from the *Major* and lit a cigarette. An oppressive silence of bewilderment lay heavily over the room.

After a long silence the *Major* resumed the conversation.

"Heilmann, I think our secret fears are proving to be true."

"You mean that it's pointless to worry your head about things, that everything's going to pot? A useless waste of our last reserves and a ridiculous *hara-kiri*."

"Umh, unfortunately..."

"You know, *Major*, I feel like a dog whose kennel's alight and who is yet too frightened to run out into the open because he's afraid of a thunderstorm..."

* * *

And then at last the orders came through for action.

In the middle of the preparations for Christmas Eve the *Kommandeur*'s telephone rang from Oldenburg ordering our immediate move to Varrelbusch.

I had no sympathy with this ridiculous jugglery, particularly as the *Staffel* Christmas Eve party would be ruined. I said so quite plainly.

"Well, I can't help it. We've got to be ready for action tomorrow in Varrelbusch."

It was pointless to argue. I felt that Weiss was also at his wits' end. So I made it short and gave the long accustomed military reply, "*Jawohl, Herr Hauptmann*", and hung up.

A short feverish consideration and then I made up my mind. The pilots should start shortly before dusk for Varrelbusch. I would remain with the rest of the staffel and follow them as the dawn broke.

I got Dortenmann to agree to this on the telephone. The same orders were given to Achmer.

In the early winter twilight of Christmas Eve the Fockes of - *Staffel* 9 taxied for the last time over the Hesepe airfield. A parting wave and they were off.

The machines roared powerfully through the dreary mist. Then the aircraft got into formation above the field, in echelon, and started their farewell circle over Hesepe which for ten long weeks had been their home. The pilots of *Staffel* 9 roared at low level for the last time over the runway then disappeared in a northerly direction.

An unusual alien silence reigned over Hesepe, and the last rays of the setting sun played on the airfield, caressing the workshops and the hangars, playing their game of shadows round the abandoned pens and tingeing the empty airfield with a waning red light.

⋆ ⋆ ⋆

Two hours later...

With loving care the village hall had been hung with flags. The bare walls had disappeared behind green pine branches. The tables, laden with food, wine and cigarettes, were arranged in a large horse-shoe. The *Stabsfeldwebel* with his party committee had taken the greatest trouble to make this Christmas Eve as beautiful as possible. The men ate their meal in joyous expectation. Many geese must have been killed before everyone finally laid down his knife and fork. The orderlies quickly cleared the tables and excited hands lit the candles of the Christmas tree.

The thoughts of all the men were with their loved ones at home.

"Stille Nacht... heilige Nacht..."

I said a few words. My speech was short and unsentimental. This wartime Christmas and its atmosphere of sorrow, the torn hearts and our burning country called for only realistic and sober phrases. The joyous message of the Christian world, that the Saviour had been born for the salvation of suffering humanity, for men leading a soldier's life tasted bitter as vinegar. Who here could believe in God, in the desperate knowledge that in their collapsing East Prussian homeland their own wives and daughters were being violated?

Who could praise God in face of the futility of endless suffering and the sacrifices of never-ending years of bitter war? They were no serfs that sat there but their fate far exceeded all possible conceptions.

Encouraging words of comradeship and of help for friends in need would be welcome; they still had some meaning.

"And we must tread this way, my friends. We all know that this is our last Christmas Eve of war, whatever happens...

"In true friendship let us make our lot more bearable...

"Like a safe protective wall round our dear country, when I joined you

'*Grünherz*' two years ago south of Leningrad the Christmas candles burnt in an enemy land.

"Our hearts belonged to our loved ones at home, our faith to the Führer and our bodies to the-Fatherland.

"This Christmas, however, the Christmas tree burns in solitude like a strangling symbol in a death-swathed land and we have no faith left. Our bodies are lost and in the end they will be damned.

"But, my friends, one thing remains to us, our hearts. Each beat shall remind us of you – mother, wife, child or father – and our thoughts are with you in this our deepest distress. Let us give a helping hand to our comrades so that our fate may be easier to bear..." I ended my speech softly. The men emptied their glasses and drank a toast to the only thing that remained to them while their country collapsed in flames and blood: "To comradeship." The red light of the candles flickered warmly over the gift table and to hide their deep emotion – some of them wiped away a furtive tear – each one summoned up a happy smile as St Nicholas with his heavy sack staggered through the door.

⋆ ⋆ ⋆

We still had to pack, although it was Christmas Eve. The light trucks of the advance guard left Malgarten. Dortenmann and I set offas dawn broke. In the cold grey light the motorised staffel column wound through the narrow streets northwards to their new airfield, Varrelbusch. The airfield lay only a few miles north of Cloppenburg.

While the ground staff column was still on the way to its new home, the fighter *Gruppe* was off on its first mission.

A magnificent picture which had not been seen for a long time. The glittering fuselages of more than eighty fighters held their course in close formation at 12,000 feet. Auxiliary fuel tanks hung like heavy bombs beneath the fuselage, for it was a long trip – over two hundred miles. The orders read: "Patrol over the front sector Liège-Nancy for low-level attacks."

We would need almost an hour, for the flight would take place at cruising speed to conserve fuel. The Fockes held their course and the compass needle showed 225°.

Below us the coal country slipped past. It depressed me to see the destruction that had taken place there. Here in the north-west of Germany no town had been spared, and worst of all was the devastation of the Ruhr.

That must be Oberhausen down there, with Borbeck next to it. A little further off lay Mülheim, a pile of ruins. Nevertheless, factory chimneys were smoking and the swirling smoke rose like a gigantic mushroom to 10,000 feet above this industrial centre.

Further to the right appeared the silver ribbon of the Rhine with Duisburg ahead, then came the first hills of the Rhineland, with the Sauerland to the north. The sky was overcast with a grey veil of cloud and mist – fog. The *Staffel* had to descend to 3,000 feet, for there was heavy "muck" ahead, travelling northwards at about thirty miles an hour. So the weather boys had given the right forecast two hours ago.

We flew over the Rhine. Over the Hocheifel things were tricky. Gigantic black clouds of basalt towered into the sky. The fighters had to adopt their bad weather formation. In flight, the Fockes always kept each other in sight. This weather was not unpleasant – perfect, in fact, for a low-level mission.

The "*Grünherz*" crossed the front below the clouds. Engines wailed, the rev. counter needles rose swiftly. Now the Fockes had to fly at least at 350 mph to avoid the ackack and to be able to dive on their intended targets.

Weapons were made ready for action, the lights in the sights switched on and already the first targets were sighted. They were Typhoons, keeping up their constant strafing of the German tanks. Weiss ordered Dortenmann, who was flying below him to port, to go down. Like hawks the Fockes of *Staffel* 8 dived on their prey.

They were far superior to the antiquated Typhoons and the battle only lasted a few minutes. Dortenmann, who had remained above his *Staffel*, watched the results with great excitement. Fourteen Typhoons had been shot down without loss.

It was incredibly sad that these tank-busters were being attacked for the first time on Christmas Day, for they had been in action since December 16th when the offensive started, and the aircraft which had halted the German tanks had mainly been Typhoons.

Me 109 *Staffel*s were in the area. We could follow them clearly on the intercom.

A cry of "Indians" warned us of a pack of Thunderbolts. Careful. Our target was now below to port.

But there was still nothing to be seen. On a broad sweep we suddenly ran into a heavy ground mist. A dangerous barrage of fiery ack-ack bursts lay ahead of our machines. We seemed to be flying above some very strong positions. Pidder Cromm, a *Leutnant* from Aachen, and Prager, who for some days had been in command of *Staffel* 10, forced their Fockes through the wall of fire. While the remaining formations watched the sky for ten minutes the two *Staffeln* pumped their ammunition into the troops below. Every available target was "pranged".

I cruised above with *Staffel* 9. Banks of cloud interfered with the visibility. Damp, grey, giant counterpanes seemed to enfold the cockpit.

A ground station tuned in. It was some advance field radio post, possibly transmitting from a tank, calling for help against a swarm of about eighty Mustangs which were carrying out lowlevel attacks on it in three waves.

A glance at the map attached to my left forearm. That must be the spot.

Ah, Weiss had already gone in with his boys.

He was on the ball. There below we could see, circling like flies, the greenish-brown checkered planes.

"Weiss to all *Staffeln*. Change over... Wade in."

Pidder Cromm broke away and twenty-one aircraft followed him in pairs.

Behind him came Dortenmann with his boys...

As is always the case in such air battles, the man who comes in from above his opponent has the advantage. The Mustangs had no spotters overhead. They had to pay for this irresponsibility and were flung into disorder.

While the *Gruppen Kommandeur* regained height with his aircraft and I took over the task of spotter, Weiss dived with his pilots on a dozen Mustangs which were trying to make a getaway.

"Make it snappy, Heilmann," came Knebe's youthful voice. "Our little friends are trying to get away."

"Too late, Kurt," I replied eagerly. The Fockes were already on the tail of the fugitives. Bursts of coloured tracers... Slim fighters cavorting, with their square radiators which hung like a fish's jaws under the fuselage. The Americans defended themselves with crazy aerobatics and yet they could not shake off the Germans. A Focke climbed in a breath-taking zoom, stalled, and spun earthwards. I looked anxiously at the diving plane. It was Yellow 9. *Feldwebel* Dehlers from BerlinWilmersdorf. The machine was too low to regain its flying speed in time. A burst of flame rose in the air confirming my fears.

Then a Mustang fleeing before two Fockes came into my sights. From barely fifty yards I pumped my death-dealing lead into the narrow fuselage. A flame spurted and the Mustang exploded like a ball of fire. I huddled in my cockpit as the debris from the wrecked Mustang hissed past me.

My *Staffel* had shot down at least seven Mustangs before Weiss gave the order for reassembly. It was time for the homeward trip, for at the beginning of the air battle some of the machines had jettisoned their auxiliary tanks and now had to go easy on their fuel if they ever wanted to get back home.

This unsound planning was a sure sign of the incapacity of High Command, for the airfields lay so far behind the scene of ops that a two-and-a-half to three-hour trip barely allowed half an hour over the front line. The reason given, that the Rhineland airfields were not to be used on account of constant enemy observation, was ridiculous and no fighter pilot believed it for one moment.

Thus at the beginning of their flight over the strongly attacked Munster Basin and the Ruhr, go per cent of the fighters became involved in tough air battles and never got to the front line because, after jettisoning their auxiliary tanks, they had not enough fuel left.

Göring indeed was waging his own war.

Five days later the fighters learned exactly why they had been posted to the north-west.

* * *

Doctor Hertel, the chief meteorologist, was saying his piece. The pilots grumbled and begged Hertel to leave them in peace.

The weather was pretty grim. Visibility was barely twenty yards and no one could tell where the sky ended and the horizon began.

That morning we had been woken up as usual. In the early light we could see nothing through the windows except a milky veil of fog. We had cheerfully gone back to bed and pulled the blankets over our heads. We slept on well into daylight...

And then orders came through to stand by, despite the impossibility of taking off in this thick ground mist.

The meteorologist fiddled nervously with his yellow hornrimmed glasses while he gave the weather forecast. "The ground mist is only local. It will disperse within the hour."

The pilots pulled wry faces. If the fog had not lifted by midday it was 99 per cent certain that it would continue throughout the afternoon.

"Snow-storms are reported over the Ruhr. You could fly round it, for the Rhineland stations report favourable flying weather. They are giving ten-tenths cloud – therefore the sky is completely overcast, with a cloud base of between 600 and 1,500 feet. Tops at 6,000."

That's no good for our bloody "crates", thought the pilots.

"Future flying conditions will become more favourable. The bad weather is passing over. The Eifel already has a visibility of between two and four miles. Over the target you will have reached the fine-weather belt. Cloud base at 3,000 feet, with gaps."

Then followed the winds, barometric pressure, etc. Doctor Hertel took his job very seriously.

The *Gruppen Kommandeur* gave his briefing and the pilots went to their aircraft where the mechanics were standing, cursing and frozen, warming up the engines.

Dortenmann, Pidder Cromm, Prager and I accompanied the *Gruppen Kommandeur* to the spot where Kiks had made his headquarters.

Hauptmann Funk, the Intelligence Officer, had just replaced the telephone on its receiver. "They're gone absolutely crackers today," he said to the new arrivals. "They've just asked, for the tenth time within the last three-quarters of an hour, if we can take off. Obviously those cretins don't believe that we're sitting in a pea soup. Hertel will confirm what I say."

"Yes, my dear Funk. It's always the same story. For weeks on end nothing, and of course one has to go on a mission on New Year's Eve because there's no time to have a good blind." Weiss grumbled away to himself as he got into his flying suit.

"*Jagdgeschwader* 26 left half an hour ago," announced Funk.

The telephone rang again shrilly.

"I'm going to cut the wires of this bastard instrument today. You just listen to what I'm going to say to them..."

"Yes, *Oberst*," said Funk, bowing slightly towards the receiver while we grinned behind his back.

"*Jawohl, Herr Oberst*. Start on our own initiative... within half an hour. Yes, sir. Unless we receive further orders. Good-bye, sir."

Funk looked breathlessly at Weiss, who was grinning; then he noticed that the rest of us were grinning too.

"What's so bloody funny about it? Oh yes. Hmm." The *Hauptmann* flicked away an imaginary speck of dust from his left tunic pocket with his finger-tips. "So... *Herr* Weiss, you're to take off despite the weather, within half an hour at the latest. You have to relieve II./JG 26. If by then the weather still makes take-off impossible we shall have to wait for new orders."

"Well, all right." Lighting a cigarette, Weiss walked over to his *Staffelkapitaen*, who were discussing the issue in front of the map. " It's not so tough, fellows. In this stinking weather we shall at least arrive over the target..."

* * *

The last machines were airborne. The *Gruppen Kommandeur* had ordered bad-weather formation, so each *Staffel* flew behind the other in echelon and set a southerly course at low level. Over the Teutoburger Wald this was highly dangerous. The cloud base was barely 150 feet above the hills. It was to be hoped that it would not grow any worse so that we would have to climb through the muck. Fighter pilots do not like blind flying. We had had plenty of training for it but the small, buoyant fighter machines made the altimeters dance and there was always too great a lag on the instruments. Anyone who flew without being calm and collected never managed to right his machine again. The instincts failed... When you thought you were flying normally, a glance at the falling altimeter and the air-speed indicator told you that the machine was plunging into a dive. If the ceiling was over 3,000 feet the pilot could not have cared less. Once he came out of the clouds he had plenty of time to pull the nose up again.

The formation slipped below a greyish black roof of bad weather. Visibility almost nil, sometimes only thirty yards over the wooden hills... You had to pay great attention to the man in front, be damned careful that his slipstream did not catch you in a whirlpool and throw you about like a withered leaf...

Visibility grew somewhat better. The dark gloomy ruins of some town glided past like a spectre. A small river and behind it a canal. That was Hamm with the Lippe Canal. It was now time to change course to starboard, for low flying over the Ruhr was impossible in this foul weather on account ofthe barrage balloons.

It began to snow heavily, taking away our last visibility. It was a hellish trip.

"Weiss calling. We must go up. Stick together or else we shall be unlucky. Keep your positions. Course 180°. Rate of climb twenty feet per second. No alteration in speed. I'll keep giving you your engine revs."

The *Gruppen Kommandeur* continued to give his many new pilots detailed and careful instructions.

My Focke flew quite peacefully in the darkness. Coldbloodedly I watched the blind-flying instruments on my panel. In such moments of danger there was no time left for unsteady nerves or else one was doomed to disaster.

An unpleasant darkness enveloped us. It must be a very thick layer of cloud. The weather boys had said 6,000 feet.

3,000... 3,300...

One must not think that at any moment a death-dealing shadow might suddenly crash into one's own machine. The perspiration broke out on my forehead.

4,500 feet...

Still the thick grey waves of fog... Ah. The wings began to be covered with milky crystals. Icing! That had to happen. Pilots were terrified of it, of its incalculability, the treacherous way that it took a machine in its grip. At any moment the ailerons and the rudder would become stiffer and stiffer as the ice gripped them. The aero-dynamics changed completely, the flying characteristics became abnormal and at a critical moment the crate dived like a winged duck.

6,000 feet...

I began to breathe more easily, for it had suddenly grown lighter. Already wisps of cloud were drifting past the cockpit like floating veils. The first dark patches crystallised out of the milky mist – the shapes of aircraft.

6,600 feet...

The first blue patches of sky appeared. The fog began to shimmer like silver and an enchanting brightness lay above. At any moment we would be out of the cloud.

7,200 feet...

A blinding whiteness made our eyes smart. The glittering clouds sped away below us and as far as the eye could see there was nothing but gleaming azure blue. The orange disc of the wintry sun lay ahead of the formation deep on the cloudy horizon. Like a grotesque, enchanted winter landscape with bizarre peaks and rising hummocks, the cotton-wool clouds lay below us. Sparkling reflections, tender green and violet shadows, golden peaks and glittering spangles.

"A miracle," I said to myself. "We actually got through it all right." Side by side in perfect formation, *Staffel* with *Staffel*, the *Gruppe* made its way to the south.

Where are we?

Weiss called the ground station and asked for a fix.

Calmly he began to count out the message. At nine it became boring and he changed over to the alphabet. Anton... Berta... Dora... Emil...

At this juncture he was interrupted. "You are in sector Ida-Siegfried 3."

Probably all the pilots were doing the same thing – looking at their maps, the squares of which were marked in green and red like a network.

Ida-Siegfried 3. Wait a moment... Oh yes, Sauerland, west of Arnsberg.

The *Gruppen Kommandeur* turned to starboard and set the new course, 230°. We flew on this course for forty-five minutes. Now we must be over the Eifel, and if, as the weather boys had prophesied, the clouds had not cleared over the front, which we would reach at the latest in fifteen

During this attack the Fw 190s were brought down by their own flak because the code warning 'Golden Rain' was received too late.

The last flight returns to the 'Grünherz' Geschwader *after an attack. Down below, black oily clouds billow up from their victims still on the ground.*

Preparing for the New Year attack on the Allied air bases in Holland and Belgium, 1945.

Heilmann's crippled Fw 190, viewed from an attacking Spitfire just before he baled out.

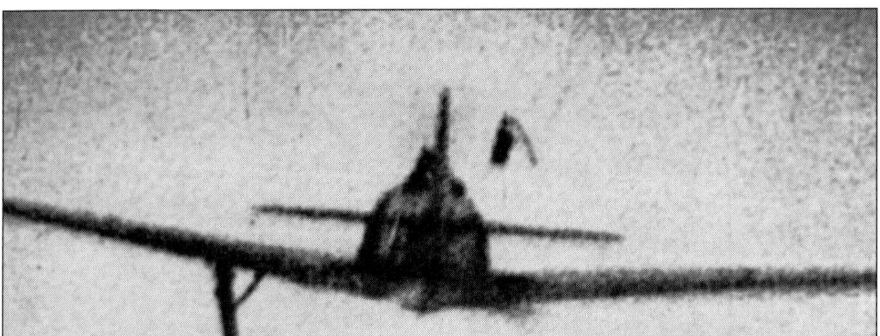

"...the next second I fell clear."

His parachute has not yet opened.

The pilotless Fw 190 turns away before crashing in flames.

Hauptmann *Robert Weiss*

Oberleutnant *Hans Dortenmann*

Leutnant *Alfred Gross*

Hauptmann *Alfred Teumer*

Oberst *Hannes Trautloft the* Kommodore *of* Jagdgeschwader *54* "Grünherz" *with his friend* Oberstleutnant *Günther Lützow,* Kommodore *of* Jagdgeschwader *3* "Udet".

Hauptmann *Nowotny and* Unteroffizier *Richter following Nowotny's last two kills on the Eastern Front. 255 Russian aircraft had fallen to his guns by 5th November 1943. After 250 victories the 22-year-old* Hauptmann *was awarded the 'Brillanten' (Diamonds). Nowotny was given command of* Jagdgeschwader *101 in Paux, southern France. The leadership of* I Gruppe *was transferred to* Hauptmann *Horst Ademeit in January 1944.*

Hauptmann *'Bully' Lang was reassigned from the* Grünherzgeschwader *on 25th July 1944 to become* Kommandeur *of II* Gruppe *of* Jagdgeschwader *26. With 144 victories, he was awarded the* 'Eichenlaub' *(Oakleaves) on 11th April 1944. Emil Lang fell on 3rd September 1944 in combat with Thunderbolts after having scored another 25 kills in the West.*

Hauptmann *Weiss with two successful piots at the Villacoublay South airbase. "Bazi" Weiss led III* Gruppe *JG 54 until he was killed in action on 29th December 1944. Weiss had scored 121 victories and was posthumously, awarded the* 'Eichenlaub' *(Oakleaves) to the Knight's Cross.*

minutes, the whole mission would be a flop, for no one was going to take the risk of diving through that muck when one didn't know where the clouds ended and the earth began.

After five minutes the first awaited dark patches appeared in the white fairyland. The further the fighters pushed westwards the more the clouds broke up and soon, through huge gaps, we could clearly see the snow-covered landscape, the dark dirty tracks of roads and rivers and then a town.

"Weiss to Cromm. Go down and see if we can safely go through the gap."

"Victor." *Staffel* 7 disappeared in steep turns through the gap.

"Cromm to Weiss. Heavy ack-ack. Follow me."

"Change course, due west. We're following."

With engines throttled back, flight after flight dived through the gap in the clouds. The cloud base was down to 1,800 feet. The bright magic of the daylight above had disappeared. The earth looked dark and gloomy under the thick canopy of clouds. We were greeted by a mad barrage of ack-ack fire. We hastened through it, westwards.

Ahead Pidder Cromm was waggling his wings.

A short breather to check our position. We must already be well behind the enemy lines. A change of course to the north. A double-track railway line ran straight ahead parallel to the river. Was it the Maas? A bombed station loomed up and then a larger town streaked past. Ack-ack. Hell, they've chosen their positions well. Two Fockes were caught in the bursts.

"Dortenmann to Weiss. That's Arlon."

So it was not the Maas. It must be a tributary.

Here we go. Eyes brightened. Tally-ho! The chase was on. There was plenty of good hunting here. A depot. A broad

field with tents and a host of huts chock full of reinforcement material of all kinds. Jeeps were loading. At the edge of the wood was a huge pile of containers.

"Let's go!"

Things were easy for the "*Grünherz*", for there was hardly any anti-aircraft defence. Taking their time and firing as if on the practice range, the Fockes destroyed their individual targets.

The deadly rain of diving and zooming machines in attack after attack lasted only five minutes. An impenetrable, ugly yellow cloud of smoke veiled the burning reinforcement camp.

Two long columns of trucks later fell a prey to the fighters. A chaos of crashed vehicles blocked the road... piles of debris.

We roared past a large village. Stop – what was that?

It was stuffed with troops.

Everywhere we could see tanks that had been hastily and badly camouflaged. This was my first attack on human dwellings. In Normandy we had always spared houses and villages but with the best will in the world it had to be different here Where tanks were parked in large numbers human interest had to take second place. It was too important a military objective and whoever had bothered about civilians in the German cities?

We left behind us a gigantic sea of flames.

Then the "*Grünherz*" flew over the front line. The cloud base there was down to 1,200 feet, and so that the fighters should not prove an easy target for the ack-ack Weiss ordered us to fly at low level.

Immediately the ground gunners went into action with red and yellow tracers.

Two machines of *Staffel* 10 were hit and crashed.

Suddenly the "*Grünherz*" found themselves involved in adog-fightwithThunderbolts. *Staffel* 9 and 10 were in the throes of a tough battle of tight turns. While Weiss hurried to the rescue with the remaining two *Staffeln*, enemy fighters dived like crazy hornets upon us from all sides.

Fuel was running low. We must get out of this scrap or else no one would reach home. Easier said than done in such a tough fight. A cry of "Tally-ho !" from Cromm. Congratulations ...At least twelve Thunderbolts and Mustangs had been brought down, but the "*Grünherz*" had received a pasting and had lost five Fockes.

I looked round for my "winger". He was still there... young Sandelmeyer. This was his first operational flight, and he had done well.

The Fockes disappeared one after the other.

The day's gone well, I thought, wiping the sweat from my face on the back of my leather glove. By now the leader must be over the Eifel.

"Look out, *Oberleutnant*. Coming in from starboard."

"Half roll. Stick to me, Sandelmeyer, otherwise you've had it." With bitter resolution my "winger" and I flew towards the six Thunderbolts, head on. The Yanks did not like that. They weakened and broke off like dogs when you stared them in the eyes.

Fire! Using both rudders to disperse the bursts, fire...

What was that? Hell! No more ammo. The belts were empty. Never mind, press on... An abominable feeling when the weapons lay there useless and nothing remained except flight and a cowardly scramble for home.

Bewildered by the hail of fire the Thunderbolts had gained height and now the two Fockes roared a few feet below them, going like mad over the valleys and hills of the Eifel. No ammunition left. Let's hope to God that nobody comes at us now from the beam.

Sandelmeyer was cursing. He was lagging behind. His engine was not pulling. It had probably received a direct hit.

"Stick on as long as you can. I'll bring you into Bonn." I had throttled back my engine and slowly the two machines glided over woods and villages towards the Rhine. By the grace of God the weather had improved.

"Watch your instruments, Sandelmeyer... Above all, your undercarriage warning light. If you're forced to land and it shows red, don't lose your nerve. You must make a crash-landing. Or if the undercarriage will only half lower and you can't get it up again you must pancake at rather more speed so that it will be shorn off."

"Victor, *Herr Oberleutnant.*"

Now we heard Weiss over the intercom. ordering us to reassemble over Cologne. So the group was still flying individually.

The Rhine. What a wonderful sight. A left-hand turn...

Flak. The crazy louts. Can't they see who we are?

"There's the airfield, Sandelmeyer. Half right and straight ahead."

I led my comrade over the Bonn-Hangelar airfield.

Sandelmeyer got away with his landing. All being well, he would fly on and join us the following morning. Hedgehopping at full speed, I pressed on alone. I must make it snappy, for the red lights had begun to flash. Careful. Only enough fuel for another quarter of an hour.

Chapter Fourteen

PRAGER, Knebe and I watched the rockets leaving the Teutoburger Wald with great excitement. The rocket trails could still be seen on the horizon. Day after day this grandiose spectacle had been repeated. In the early morning or just before midday, but mostly of an evening, these trails of smoke zigzagged through the sky. A brilliant red flame turned swiftly into a yellowish white column of smoke. For almost a minute the image remained on the horizon. One could clearly recognise the path of the rockets as they began their guided course.

"So that's the V-2," said Kurt Knebe thoughtfully. The three of us were on our way through a pine wood to get a goose for Knebe's girl-friend.

"Well, it was high time we got something else. The V-1 doesn't worry the British any more," said Prager. He had never stopped grousing since his arrival in Varrelbusch. Nothing escaped his criticism and any hopes of the promised miracle he "had long put to bed to let the moths get at it", as he said with a bitter smile.

"Have a look at that one. It's going off the beam." I pointed excitedly to a trail of fire which, instead of rising vertically as usual, had curved away at an angle of 30° towards the Rhine.

"I'll tell you something, Willi. That must be a pretty lousy outfit to be in. I shouldn't like to be one of the men in that type of experimental group. I'd rather have our circus."

"Rubbish, Kurt. When about ten to twenty tons of explosive goes off you don't feel it any more. It's over too quickly, far quicker than when one of our chaps stops one in his cockpit."

"How high do you think those things go?" asked Knebe.

I made a small calculation.

"It's simply a matter of triangles, as old Papa Glenz taught me God knows how many years ago at school. It's quite simple. From here to Teuto is about sixty miles. The highest still visible smoke trail" – I stretched out my right arm to form the triangle – "lies over there. So from my shoulder it makes an angle of about 40°. As we should have a right-angled triangle with the length of one side and one angle known (in addition to the right angle) the height over there must be about thirty-five miles."

"Hell's bells!" whistled Prager through his teeth. I didn't know whether his whistle was in admiration of my mathematics or surprise at the colossal height of the rocket.

"Look," I said, "the V-2 is shot over sixty miles vertically into the air. Then it flattens out and is guided from the ground to its target and it falls when it has reached that target – at least in theory."

"Good God. It must be terrible. No air-raid precautions can cope with that... not even an alert... there seems to be no possible defence. And they still go on fishing peacefully in the Thames."

"You're confusing London with Paris, old man. The English are not a bit like the Froggies, who will sit fishing for hours on end by the Seine without catching anything." Knebe's boyish laughter rang out as he banged Prager on the shoulder.

"I couldn't care bloody less, Kurt, if they go fishing or not, or whether they go on the spree round Piccadilly Circus or whatever the damned place is called... but suddenly the V-2 arrives and you've had your chips. Death falls out of a clear sky and an area of perhaps a few hundred square yards is simply blotted out, so from one minute to the next..."

"But that's not the worst, Heini. The brain has no time to take it in. But just think of the eternal hideous terror, the appalling uncertainty. When's the next one coming and where's it going to fall? "

"To hell with that, Willi. Why should we worry? Just look what they've done for years to the Ruhr. Just come home with me and see what life's like there. Sirens wailing non-stop, constant rushing from shelter to work and then back to the shelter. You should have a taste of it some time." Heini Prager lashed the grass angrily with his knobbly stick, making the snow fly.

By now we had left the wood. It was not much farther to the poultry farm. Knebe went on ahead and Prager and I said that we would wait for him.

"You know, Prager, all this doesn't amuse me any more. It's pure murder... ruthless, vile destruction that we're sending over there. The times of real soldiering, of manliness, honour and duty have gone for ever. Look, we soldiers have wagered our lives and our blood to wrest a place in the sun once more for Germany, something the other world powers wanted to prevent. To help the Fatherland acquire fame and wealth; to make it large and strong so that it could become a flourishing well-run country guaranteeing our families a decent future.

"And as an officer I'm supposed to give the men a shining example so that they should follow me in true and loyal comradeship. But that... hell, no...

"Modern warfare is nothing more than a flail of terror. As long as it remains in the front line I've nothing to say against it, for the mailed fist must always fight for rights which can never be won with intellectual and moral weapons, but murder shouldn't be carried into the hinterland. We went into the war to protect women and children, a task that men have always undertaken ever since there were men, but it is a loathsome and disgraceful act to murder the enemy's women and children and to burn his houses and homes...

"I can't help it, Heini, but I don't want to have anything more to do with it. I loathe this mass murder, and hatred knows no bounds. Anyone who wants to remain a decent human being and to save his soul must scream it to the house-tops, no more war."

"Do you think I don't feel the same? A great chance has come about. Suppose one of us had said that two or three years ago."

"You're right, my friend. In those days I was an eager student of Clausewitz and the other great military experts. But Clausewitz may have been right. He certainly was for his own period, when he said that war is the father of all things.

"As things have turned out today, I should like to say only this gruesome ordeal can lead the peoples of the world towards peace. The conqueror will in fact be almost as poor as the conquered, and human intelligence will perhaps have time to realise that men must seek their life's work in solving common economical problems."

"You are an incorrigible idealist, Willi. I hold out little hope. Even in the time of the mercenaries the slogan *The survivor is always right* held good. And I hope that you will survive to the end of this war to see how the Bolshies, the Yanks and the Tommies will swing the whip of victory. Adolf will be dead then and all those responsible wiped out. The people can drink the brew they have concocted. But whoever still believes in right, God and peace will be a bloody fool."

"Unfortunately, you're probably right. What will happen at the end of the war? They will betray us until the cock has crowed thrice. Respect for honour dies with honour, reverence dies with fear and all the temples collapse. We soldiers will be greeted with words of shame and reproach. The victors will do that and our own people will defame us through the mouths of their new government. 'You wanted it that way,' they will say to us with a sneer. Down with the uniforms. Tear off your orders and decorations.

"People will be only too pleased to grab from us the symbols of an exhausting struggle, of suffering and death, and woe to the poorest of us that has to remain in custody among men who will be thirsting for revenge.

"The slave traffic of the old days will be revived. No man is the property of another except of his own accord. That's called the 'Rights of Man', isn't it?"

"But again, woe betide the man who has the courage to voice his own opinion. He can be compared with a madman striding through a robber-infested wood at night with a lighted candle.

"We shall be slung into some corner of our ruined towns to squat and starve. A dreadful spiritual confusion will make it impossible to believe any longer in the dignity of man.

"Under the infernal searchlight beams of revenge each of us will have to find his own way alone like a wanderer lost in the forest, cleaving a path through the jungle vegetation with his axe, halting from time to time and listening attentively for the faint far-off sounds which prove to him that others are on the same path as himself.

"I ask you, after all our suffering, death and endurance, have we soldiers really deserved that?"

My words came stertorously to the surface as though through a thick layer of oil.

"Do as I do, Willi. Enjoy life to the full. On the one side death and on the other in one's spare moment's exuberant glittering life. You often frowned, old chap, when I acted too crazily... but be fair. Aren't I right to grab everything that the world can possibly give me? If we come to grief, let's go down with our flags flying, with all the stops of the organ out until the bloody thing explodes."

At that moment Knebe came running up with a goose under his arm. With his right hand he forced the birds' beak shut so that its quacking should not betray its presence to any stranger's ears.

Darkness lay over the wood as we made our way back home. We hurried into Barten's hut where the bird was to be killed. To our amusement we found our friend asleep.

"Hush," said Prager, putting his forefinger to his lips. "Put the light out."

He placed the goose on Barten's chest. In its new-won freedom the frightened bird quacked with excitement, waddled over the sleeping man's face and started flapping its wings furiously. Such a din would have awakened the dead.

There was a gurgling scream. I suddenly switched on the light. The goose was fluttering with wild cries all over the bed.

Barten-Foss was as white as a sheet. "How the hell could you do such a thing? You nearly frightened me to death."

"Here, have a schnapps, otherwise you'll pass out." We laughed so much that the *Oberleutnant*'s temper gradually subsided.

At last Knebe drew his jack-knife and killed the goose. He was quite an expert at this job.

It turned out to be the last meal of roast goose for *Oberleutnant* Barten-Foss, who was brought down next day in a battle with Spitfires over Rheine.

⋆ ⋆ ⋆

The bus that drove the pilots to the airfield that winter morning of the 29th December had its windows covered with ice. Nature had decked the landscape with its magic wand and there was a bright display of ice crystals.

Overnight it had become bitterly cold. A high-pressure belt from the Azores the night before had entered north-west Germany which had lain for weeks under a depression. A cold clear winter day broke, and as the pale sun rose to the southeast over the Kloppenburg forests, a white snowy landscape glowed with a wonderful mixture of tints from dark red to golden yellow and bluish white. A dark-blue sky lay over the pine forests. The slender trees were covered with thick clumps of snow and a fresh morning wind played dreamily in their white hoods. A rain of gold fell from them...

Early in the morning ops started in earnest. The orders were massed *Staffeln* flights, for enemy formations had been reported in small groups distributed over a wide area. Once more it was the usual fighter-bomber attacks by the checker-board Thunderbolts and the red-nosed Mustangs – both of them old acquaintances of the "*Grünherz*".

Staffel 7 and 10 had already flown their mission. After achieving some success they returned to the Osnabruck sector.

The midday sun stood high and its rays reflected a thousandfold from the bright, snow-dazzled Rheine.

Dortenmann was in his cockpit ready to take off and was only waiting for the order to start. New fighter-bomber attacks were reported in the Dortmund-Rheine area.

Outside headquarters stood the *Gruppen Kommandeur* and I with my gang, and the officers of the radio staff. At that moment formations of four-engined bombers were reported over the Dutch coast. Weiss looked gravely at his officers and we knew that this beautiful sunny day would prove a hard ordeal for us. No sign of a cloud that might serve as cover.

Orders came through for the "*Grünherz*" over the loudspeaker. Weiss seized the 'Very' pistol, opened a window and fired a green flare – the signal for Dortenmann to take off.

Engines wailed, propeller slipstreams threw up whirlwinds of snow behind the aircraft. The machines roared over the field towards headquarters.

All the officers there looked up in amazement. *Hauptmann* Funk had just shouted excitedly, "Indians over the field!"

Everyone ran to the window anxious to see the fun. The small black dots grew larger at every moment in the midday sun. Weiss had grabbed the earphones.

"Weiss to Dortenmann. Low-level attack behind the flak positions. You've got Indians on your tail."

Too late. In the next moment the wild chase began. Mustangs, our old foes with the red noses, about thirty of them...

The flak gunners fired with everything they had got. The fight for the tightest turns began. Near the ground machines were flung about with mad zooms, giddy rolls and climbing turns to stalling point to wrest the advantage from the enemy.

From below we looked with dark faces at the gruesome game being played above the giant arena. Weiss continued to give instructions over radio but he could not do very much. Up there, every pilot held his fate in his own hands.

Three Mustangs lay burning on the "deck", but four Fockes had flown their last flight. No possibility of baling out so near the ground. Bodies would have been smashed to pieces by the crashing aircraft.

Red 1, Dortenmann, streaked over the airfield forcing down a Mustang that was taking desperate avoiding action. Now Dortenmann was firing... The Mustang made a last effort to get away and crashed at full speed into the fuel dump. An enormous column of flame... A few seconds later it was rising a hundred feet high above the edge of the airfield.

Dortenmann waggled his wings as a sign of victory. Then he had to defend himself, for three pursuers were on his tail as he banked in the opposite direction.

The veteran pilot kept his head. A sharp zoom and at giddy speed he side-slipped across the field. The enemy was now right on his beam.

Those of us below held our breath. If only things went well now... but he must pull it off. If he wanted to get away with his life he must have a shot at a breakneck landing.

The three Mustangs followed him down. They wanted to shoot him out of the sky while he was attempting his forced landing. Keep your fingers crossed that he pulls it off...

Dortenmann touched down and the Focke leaped into the air again like an enraged buck; but he was an old hand at the game and he forced his Focke down on to the deck. It held as far as the edge of the field leaving a three hundred yard long black trail in the white snow before it began to burn.

Dortenmann's pals breathed with relief when he jumped out and took a header into a trench, where he was safe from the tracers of the attacking Mustangs.

It was a bad start to the day. From the nearby airfield badly damaged Fockes landed in all directions. They had been badly shot up. Four Mustangs had crashed but five men were dead from *Staffel* 8. Two wounded pilots had to be sent to hospital in Kloppenburg. Dortenmann had a flesh wound on his left upper arm.

I took off half an hour later with *Staffel* 9. We flew eastwards towards the Dummer See to meet the oncoming four-engined bomber stream. This would surely entail a scrap. Climbing to 18,000 feet, I changed course to the west. Soon we caught sight of the approaching enemy fighters. Six to ten thousand feet below us glittered wave after wave, the advance guard. In a few moments the four-engined bombers would appear.

"Leading bomber formation over Wesel," quacked the RT. Shortly afterwards we received the order to make for Rheine where fighter-bombers were still on the job.

I changed the course to the south above the Ems moors. In a matter of moments we would be at Rheine. Knebe reported that he was going down as his engine had oiled up.

"Keep your eyes skinned, Kurt," I called to him over the intercom. As Knebe broke away we could all see the black oily stains on his windscreen. That definitely put him out of the fight.

Rheine. The station stood out clearly.

A dozens shadows circled far below the Fockes. The well-known outlines of Mustangs. They could be recognised by their crucifix shape, with the wings the same size as the body. In aircraft-recognition lectures they were familiarly known as "Flying Crosses".

"Heilmann to Ostro. Remain aloft with the main body and protect our rear."

I broke away and eighteen machines followed me down to the attack. The Mustang pilots were lynx-eyed and recognised their foe immediately. They hastily formed into a defence circle.

We know all about that, I thought. Now they'll call for help. We must get this over and done with in five minutes at the latest or else they'll tie us up in knots.

My *Staffel* managed to break the defence circle at the first attack. Two Mustangs spun to earth. Then the dog-fight began...

I called in Patt. This new attack from above sowed confusion among the Mustangs. For a moment they lost their nerve. Two more were set on fire and broke off the engagement. Then a third column of flame rose below from a near farm. The remaining seven machines careered about wildly in their attempt to shake off their pursuers who were now superior in numbers.

The Fockes were faster and clung on, firing desperately into the machines, into the black smoke which denoted that they were flat out. Another Mustang caught fire.

I banked and gave orders for my men to regroup.

Not a single machine lost! Despite our superiority in numbers this was by no means inevitable. We flew low over the place where the Mustangs had crashed. The men waved. It was a picture the fighters liked to see, for only too seldom did they see signs of their success blazing on the ground. I announced that I was making for Varrelbusch.

"Hang on a bit," I was told. "Things are sticky here. If you don't hear from us land at Vechta."

"Nice of you to say so. The sky there's full of 'crates'."

We had hardly left Rheine behind us than enemy machines appeared from both sides – Spitfires and Tempests. I felt desperately afraid. This is going to be a damned hard nut to crack, I thought.

"Heilmann to all pilots. Look out, Tempests in the air. Keep formation, we're faster than they are. Tight turns and gain height."

Soon we were in a hurricane of fire. In this battle for position the Fockes were forced down slightly. There were about twenty Spitfires and at least a dozen Tempests. The Focke pilots fought desperately in their attempt to gain height. *Leutnant* Schmerzer was sticking too close to my tail. In a dangerously narrow turn to avoid a collision he flew right into the line of fire which was really intended for me. He caught fire and pulled up his nose. Then he screamed pathetically over the intercom, for help.

"Bale out, boy," I gasped, defending myself from two Tempests. "I can't get in any closer..." Schmerzer's Focke fell into a spin with a long trail of flame streaming from behind it.

Weaving desperately, I dived below the trees, almost grazing the hedges, and streaked away to the north. A brief respite... For the moment I was alone. Outside a village lay an undamaged Spitfire; men were running from all sides to catch the fleeing pilot.

Flying as low as I could I skirted a long strip of wood... With a start of terror I had to zoom... A Focke sped across my track followed by two Tempests.

I yanked my machine round to get on their tails. Supercharger in action, the Focke shivered and vibrated while my pal ahead banked sharply to port. The two Tempests followed but their turns were too wide and they lost distance. In the excitement of the chase the British had not noticed me. I zoomed... did a half roll and a dive. Now I had cut off one Tempest. Great stuff. The rear machine came into my sights. I yanked the stick so wildly that condensation appeared on the wings and I had a blackout. "For Christ's sake fire at him," came over the intercom. "Can't you see I'm trying to keep straight?"

I pressed the firing button. A long burst... The tracers flew past the enemy's tail. The pilot of the Tempest had at last spotted his new enemy, did a half roll and turned away to starboard. He was crazy... He flew straight into my line of fire.

"Nice work. Now let's dispose of the other one together."

"What a nerve! That can only be Prager or Patt, eh?"

"No, it's Father Christmas !" came the reply. Now we caught the second Tempest in our pincers but the Britisher would not play and streaked away with his faster machine.

The two Fockes closed into formation.

Prager waved. "Nice job you did, Willi. I didn't know how the hell to get rid of those two."

"The next time I hope you're there, Heini, to do the same for me."

We were now flying wing tip to wing tip, and we hedgehopped to a nearby airfield.

We had to circle the field, for nine aircraft were just taking off. They were the *Gruppen Kommandeur*'s flight with the green numbers.

"Heilmann to Weiss. Good luck and good hunting."

"Thanks, Willi, and congratulations."

While the *Gruppen Kommandeur* took off in a southerly direction, Prager and I landed.

We were the last. We would wait for the other missing machines in vain. Out of the twenty-two who had been in the dog-fight, seven were brought down that afternoon by the enemy. The pilots were all killed. Among them where *Oberleutnant* Barten-Foss, *Leutnant* Schmerzer and *Feldwebel* Raschel from Mannheim.

Still slightly out of breath Prager and I arrived at headquarters. Dortenmann was there, with his left arm in a sling.

"What goes on? Why are you all looking so grim?" I asked.

Neumann said slowly, "Weiss is in bad trouble in a bloody awful air battle over Rheine. They seem to have caught up with a huge formation of Spitfires."

After two minutes silence reigned in the loudspeaker after the mad chaos. Kiks kept calling in vain. *Hauptmann* Funk was very pale and kept looking at everyone with eyes full of misery. Then he pushed Kiks out of the way and put his mouth close to the mouthpiece. "Robert, Robert." His fists were clenched and his hands were shaking. The tension was unbearable. "Robert Robert,..." Nothing but a slight splutter in the loudspeaker. "He must have forgotten to plug in his radio," he said, turning to the others with tears in his eyes. Funk could not imagine that anything could have happened to Robert Weiss. No one would believe it. This terrible 29th December had already claimed enough victims from the "*Grünherz*".

The group waited in vain for their *Gruppen Kommandeur* and his *Staffel* to return. Not far from Rheine they found the debris and ashes of the aircraft. The bodies were almost unrecognizable

Hauptmann Robert Weiss, a very brave man and the much-beloved *Kommandeur* of III./*Jadgeschwader* 54, who had won the oak leaves with swords several weeks before, had found a pilot's death, and with him eight pilots of his own *Gruppe*, *Hauptmann* Boitcher, *Hauptmann* Timge, *Leutnants* Ratzleff, Denker, Minsen and Feller; Pilot Officer Jongen, *Gefreiter* Karzenau. All these nine machines which had been sent to Rheine were a certain prey for the vastly superior Spitfire formations.

A few days later an Order of the Day came through and was read out to the group. It referred to this brave Viennese who, with his "*Grünherz*" *Gruppe*, had to his credit the greatest number of victories on the invasion front.

But these words could not atone, for they came far too late – and they were almost as futile and meaningless as had been the order that flung these fighters in single staffels into the teeming hosts of enemy aircraft in a brilliant blue sky.

Chapter Fifteen

I TOOK over the *Gruppe* after Robert Weiss had been killed. The pilots tore themselves out of the deep depression into which they had fallen since that disastrous 20th December In any case they were given little time for grief or reflection. In a mad chaos, mission followed upon mission. Only during the first few days of the New Year did it grow quieter, for the weather had changed and heavy snow-storms made take-off impossible. Nevertheless an alert was given in the middle of our preparations for the New Year's Eve party and at about four o'clock in the afternoon we were given orders to take off.

Everyone was furious and we grumbled quite openly. To outward appearances the order looked completely stupid, a mere bit of staff imbecility, for it was almost impossible to fly – bad visibility, low cloud, a gusty wind and it would be dark within the hour.

Then it began to snow and our cup was full...

I was so angry that I felt inclined to disobey orders. I reported on the telephone the number of machines that were airworthy. Was it absolutely essential that they should fly and if so must I send the whole *Gruppe*?...

I might have saved myself the trouble. The result: I received a rocket from my superior and the strict orders that all airworthy machines of the *Gruppe* must take off.

Sixty Fockes took off in the grey twilight. In this snowstorm, a long period of circling over the airfield was necessary until all the machines were in good formation position. The order came through from the ground station "Course I80°." Nothing else. What a strange thing. No weather report and no target...

Visibility was so bad that we naturally had to fly in bad weather formation. The staffels flew behind each other in order to avoid collision. The "*Grünherz*" were now between

the slopes and deep valleys of the Teutoburger Wald. At low altitude sixty pilots were risking their lives, for all the hilltops were covered with cloud.

Slowly the twilight enveloped the country...

Windscreen wipers began to hum as they swept the snow from the windscreens.

I could see about five machines round me. The same thing must apply to all the others... As we were flying so low, we were unable to make radio contact with ground control. Pidder Cromm swore like a trooper. Dortenmann raged. Prager even swore that he would dive his "crate" into the muck if this bloody stupidity lasted much longer.

I warned the pilots to observe the greatest caution. Anyone who by chance saw the possibility of landing should land straight away.

It grew still darker in the driving snow. It was now impossible to get back to our own airfield. We would have to turn onto our opposite course. To try the manvouvre with a formation of sixty machines and little more than a hundred feet above the ground in this narrow valley which seemed to lurk there like a mousetrap was pure lunacy, suicide.

A nice New Year's present!

A ball of flame lit up the snow. One of *Staffel* 10 must have hit the deck. Another casualty then.

I was overcome by an irresistible and impotent rage. If only those half-wits who had cooked this up for us were here and had broken their bloody necks instead of that poor bastard. Crazy murderers sending people off in this filthy weather. There can't possibly be any enemy formations in the region, so what's the point of it?

Suddenly I recognised below the network of the Mitteland Canal. Now I knew where we were.

"Heilmann to Dortenmann. That's Hopsten below us.

"Circle slowly in a right-hand turn. Keep as high as possible. Dortenmann land immediately," I ordered.

Staffel after *Staffel* landed. In the semi-darkness and as a result of bad nerves and the danger of the situation there were many crash landings. Fifty-two machines landed safely in the course of one minute. One of the pilots was dead, as we already knew. It was to be hoped that nothing had happened to the other seven although no one yet knew their fate.

"Right, we'll collect the aircraft tomorrow morning. Call up the airfield and tell them to send a bus. We'll drown our sorrows in drink and have a good New Year's Eve party, eh?"

Cursing and blinding, we stamped our feet in our heavy fur-lined boots in the snow. Then we made our way to the mess.

"Get on to Varrelbusch," Prager ordered one of the *Gefreiters*. With an embarrassed look on his face the man stammered that he had strict orders not to use the phone.

"Is there a raid going on or something?"

"It's the bloody limit."

The four of us were discussing matters excitedly when we were interrupted by a *Hauptmann* who had just come in.

"I'm Worner," he said, introducing himself.

He was in command of II./JG 26 stationed at Hopsten. With a bitter-sweet expression he told us that we would have to spend New Year's Eve with him – "But I'm afraid there's no drink, gentlemen," he added.

And then we learned the reason for this crazy breakneck mission. We were to be away from Varrelbusch that night. All the airfields here since midday had been crammed full of fighters like sardines in a tin. The more distant fighter staffels such as the "*Grünherz*" in Varrelbusch were to be centralised. The order to land was to have been given to us once we were airborne, but since we were flying at low level the ground station could not get in touch with us.

"And so, hypnotised by some strange telepathic waves, we came on our own initiative and landed in Hopsten," I said with a laugh. "But can you tell me the reason for all this, *Hauptmann*?"

"Come over to my quarters please, gentlemen."

A little later we entered an attractive room in the house of a local innkeeper on the edge of the airfield. *Hauptmann* Worner asked my friends and I to sit down.

"Gentlemen, I have here a sealed envelope but I am not allowed to open it until three o'clock tomorrow morning, so you see I haven't the slightest idea myself what sort of New Year's present they've sent us. I can only tell you one thing, that you and your staff are under no circumstances to get in touch with anyone outside this airfield.

"Secondly, there are to be no New Year's Eve celebrations.

"And thirdly, may I invite you all to supper? It is actually ready now and in an hour's time everyone will be off duty including all the officers."

Dortenmann whistled through his teeth. "Hell's bells! So it must have been all thought out without anyone giving us an inkling of what was happening."

Prager ground his teeth and shook his mop of hair angrily. With resignation he thought of the girl who was now waiting in vain for him – a girl who had come all the way from Hesepe for New Year's Eve and was now waiting in Varrelbusch.

* * *

Quite a decent meal was waiting for us on the table.

No one spoke a word, for the shock we had just suffered had been too great.

Even the jokers in the company stared at the food in front of them and replied in monosyllables.

Patt alone managed to lighten the mood somewhat. At the end of the meal he asked my permission to speak. With a mournful vinegary face he grabbed his glass of milk – as a result of the ban on alcohol, pilots were only allowed to drink soda water, milk or coffee – and, blinking meaningly at the silent assembly, he announced curtly "I must now act as toast master. Well, Prosit and let's hope we'll have a better New Year."

Faces broke out into wry grins. Then we saw the funny side of it and began to laugh. Patt's New Year's speech had finally relieved the tension.

★ ★ ★

An hour later we were all asleep – or at least trying to sleep, for who could possibly go to bed on New Year's Eve at such an early hour? It was only seven o'clock in the evening. We knew that something unusual was afoot and that on the following day a number of us must die.

We were woken at three o'clock in the morning and half an hour later all the pilots of *Jagdgeschwader* 26 and III./JG 54 were assembled in the messroom. *Hauptmann* Worner came in with the ominous envelope already open in his hand.

"To make it brief, boys, we're taking off with more than a thousand fighters at the crack of dawn to prang various airfields on the Dutch-Belgian border.

A magnificent New Year's Eve present, indeed!

Then followed details of take-off, flying order, targets and return flights. The communiques of the security service were read out giving precise details of the positions of the enemy airfields and the particularly heavy ack-ack strongpoints behind the enemy's lines.

Brussels was the target for III./JG 54.

The pilots were given accurate maps and particularly worthwhile targets were pointed out to them. The formations were to fly in close consecutive waves led by fast pathfinders over the North Sea and then to make a wide sweep to port until they reached the Dutch coast. After that they would have to find their own directions, for by that time it would be light enough.

The whole mission was to be carried out at less than 600 feet until they reached the targets so that the enemy ground stations could not pick them up. To this end radio silence was the order until they reached the target.

★ ★ ★

We were given a magnificent breakfast.

Was it a New Year's feast or the last meal of a condemned man?

Cutlets, roast beef and a glass of wine. For sweets there were pastries and several cups of fragrant coffee. The iron rations were handed out – two bars of chocolate and some glucose tablets.

The last minutes before we were airborne seemed an eternity. Nervous fingers stubbed out half-smoked cigarettes.

I gave my final instructions to the *Staffelkapitaen* and then went over to join my pilots of *Staffel* 9. If they lost contact they were to join some other formation immediately. Only in absolute necessity were they to turn eastwards and fly back alone – at the lowest possible level. It would be easy enough to spot the Rhine.

And then the armada took off....

A distant roar in the air soon increased in strength. Soon the pathfinder aircraft were circling above the field which was now brightly lit up.

Machine after machine took off, circled and regrouped. *Staffel* after *Staffel* set out. Far ahead the navigating lights of the leading pathfinders twinkled in the early dawn.

Things went off as planned. Over the sea the pathfinders turned off to the left and the staffels flew round on to a southern course. But the addle-pated High Command had forgotten one thing – or else they had purposely omitted it on security grounds – to notify their own anti-aircraft.

Although the fighters fired their recognition flares, a crazy flak barrage claimed its first victim over the coast. How on earth were they expected to recognise the aircraft?

In a scarlet glow the sun appeared slowly above the horizon to the east.

It was 8.25 a.m.

After crossing the flak barrage we flew in peace. No ack-ack, no fighters... Completely unsuspecting, the allied troops were sleeping off their New Year's parties, nursing their thick heads without the remotest idea of the storm that was already brewing over their heads.

My *Staffel* was in the first wave. We surprised the few sentries and ack-ack crews. Far astern rose the scarlet tracer fingers seeking out the later waves of aircraft.

So many German fighters had never yet been sent out on one mission. It was an overwhelming sight which for a long time had only been seen on the enemy's side.

The first targets were reached.

Curt orders over the intercom.; splitting up of the individual formations. Soon the first wave was over Brussels.

The calm of a New Year's morning still lay over the sleeping city. The towers and gables glittered a golden red in the early sunlight. The famous Grande Place with its proud business and patrician houses – I had often visited it – sped past. A few moments later we had crossed the outskirts of the city and had reached our target – the big airfield of Haren.

It was plastered with aircraft as we could see at once. Long rows of uncamouflaged four-engine bombers, for the most part Boeings, stood on the airfield. On the opposite side of the field to the north were scores of fighters.

Why should they have bothered to camouflage them?

The Germans never came as far as this – the damned bandits. They never took to the air.

And yet here we were! In pyjamas, vests and pants the gunners rushed to their positions.

"Let's go! Tally-ho!"

Within five minutes the whole airfield with aircraft, fuel tanks, workshops and buildings, had been turned into a smouldering scrap-heap. In a panic, the pilots and ground staff, barefooted and in pyjamas, rushed through the snow and tumbled head over heels into any spot of cover they could find.

"OK, boys! That makes it quits. How often have you made us dance to this tune? As courteous people it was high time we paid you a return visit." I smiled grimly, as I observed the panic down below. Then I gave the order "Regroup" and soon all my men had closed in on the leader's machine that was waggling its wings. A swift glance behind me. A11 of them seemed to have joined me, thank God. One more glance at the smoking pile of debris and the occasional columns of flames. The snow had melted and dirty grey pools of water had formed between the burning aircraft. One solitary ack-ack crew fired in vain at the "*Grünherz*" as we left.

For the next week things would be deathly quiet here. The aircraft had flown their last missions and would never drop their tons of death and destruction on Germany. There must have been about sixty four-engined bombers and hundreds of fighters.

If all the *staffeln* had been as successful as we had, then this New Year's visit would have been an unqualified success.

The old familiar black puffs now burst beneath our aircraft. A heavy ack-ack barrage of iron and flame. They had woken up now below and their rude awakening had transformed the whole country into an angry wasp's nest.

We winged our way homewards at low level. Dortenmann went upstairs with his *staffel* to cover us from above. Five minutes later he called for help. Spitfires had attacked him over Hasselt. So they had already got the news in England! Now came the toughest part of the journey for the staffels who were still deep in enemy country.

I went to the rescue and spiralled up with three *Staffeln* to join Dortenmann who had reported his altitude as 5,000 feet.

"Heilmann calling. Hold on, we're coming."

Steep upward spirals. 3,000... 3,500... 4,000... 6,000.

"There they are, right below us." Pidder Cromm broke away, followed by Prager's *Staffel*. There were about forty Spitfires. I'll wait a bit, I thought, closely following the battle in order to choose the best moment for attacking. Everything went well. The Spitfire was the most dangerous of all aircraft in merry-go-round tactics. With their oval pointed wings they made incredibly tight turns. Nevertheless three of them had already been shot down and a Focke caught fire a moment later.

This is it!

The last twenty Fockes dived like a flash of lightning into the battle. The British weakened and to their satisfaction the German fighters for once saw Spitfires in flight. A dozen crashed machines were burning below the scene of the battle.

"Let them go. We must get home or else we shan't have enough juice."

The Fockes dived away and began to hedge-hop over woods and hedges, villages, canals and gun positions. The ack-ack gunners spotted their enemy too late even though the alert had been sent to all stations.

Suddenly the firing ceased. There was a deep satisfying silence. The flat meadows of the Lower Rhine sped past below us... hedges, meadows, villages, and there was the Rhine.

The pilots waved cheerfully to each other. They had come to life again.

Now we could celebrate New Year's day.

The Luftwaffe Command must have had the bright idea that people all over the world liked to celebrate the New Year. Next day there were no operations.

* * *

The success of this famous attack on the airfields in the Dutch-Belgian sector was very great but it was quite rightly criticised. The enemy had suffered a heavy and painful defeat, but only in material. Within fourteen days they would have made good these losses.

But what of the German fighter arm?

The losses it suffered were never published. Even the gentlemen of the Fighter General Staff had not the least idea. People knew that certain wings had suffered terribly, particularly those who had brought up the rear.

The "*Grünherz*" got home safely but they had been flying in the first wave. Only *Oberfeldwedel* Knell had to make a forced landing. The German flak shot him down near Rotterdam and he was taken to hospital with serious burns.

During the attack three aircraft were lost and six Fockes were brought down in the dog-fight over Hasselt but this was well above expectations.

Later, individual unit commanders complained that the armada had lost about 30 per cent of its original strength. That was a very high figure.

In Germany men were now more important than machines and losses could no longer be made good now that good pilots had become a great rarity.

Chapter Sixteen

A TREMOR ran through the hand with all the sinews taut, clutching the control column in a vice-like grip... and with a shudder it seemed to grope in the blue and then fell back between the knees.

For a few seconds the stick remained vibrating in a central position, then it jolted and wobbled as though lashed by an invisible flail, forward and to the left, jerked slowly backwards... remained stationary for a moment. The next instant it fluttered helplessly in light zigzags to and fro, as though confused....

After a few seconds the same game was repeated.

This was the reverse of the normal joystick movements of an aircraft. Strong, sinewy hands manocuvre the stick, making the elevators and ailerons respond; the aircraft must obey its pilot.

Now, however, the pilot hung unconscious in his straps. In the whirlwind dog-fight the Focke had obeyed the slightest pressure on the controls but now it had run riot.

A vicious stream of air pressed against the rudder. Pilotless... out of control... at the behest of the wind....

Suddenly, like a shot stag, the machine toppled over on its left wing. There were twenty-four white victory marks on the fuselage.

And now it began to spin slowly down to the ground.

The pilot's head wobbled weakly from side to side almost following the mad wobble of the control column. Deep lines could be seen on the cramped ashen face still betraying, even in this painless unconsciousness, the desperate efforts that had been made during his panic.

The leather flying helmet had been torn from his forehead. A broad, tight band had left the sweat-drenched black hair free. A small, ugly trickle of blood ran down from the left eye over the chalky-white cheek.

The machine spun inexorably earthwards.

Closer and closer rose the earth... after the thaw of the previous days it had become green, red and brown once more, gleaming in the bright sunshine. The world revolved beneath the spinning aircraft like a gigantic infinite merry-go-round.

The Focke was now cold, dead metal.

Not quite, however. It had a heart and a brain. The engine and the electrical equipment enjoyed their own life and their own field of energy. Every pilot knows this and respects and spares his Focke, to whose enormous engine power and elegant pirouettes he entrusts his life.

In timorous, fluttering circles the Focke spun deeper and deeper. My trusty Yellow 6.

"Alas, my friend," it seemed to say," that is all I can do for you if you leave my controls free. I cannot fly without your hand to guide me. Long ago by rights we should have been smashed to pieces, but see how I am trying to help. I'm spinning as flat as possible. From 21,000 feet it takes a long time at this rate and as a dumb machine I can do no more. But hurry, pilot. Shake from your brow the darkness of death which has you in its spell. Give me your hand and we'll get out of the frying-pan which has flung you dangerously near the fire. Wake up!"

Threateningly, Yellow 6 bucked and jerked in the slipstream. My head wobbled faster to and fro and hit the left wall of the cockpit with a bump.

A groan of pain was wrung from my compressed lips. My limbs stretched and my blood-stained eyelids made an effort to open. Then my limbs sank back into their torpor. My left hand unwittingly touched the throttle and pushed it forward. The engine picked up at once. "That's better, pilot. Carry on." With a wail of its 2,000 horse-power the Focke put on speed. The control column was lashed backwards and hit hard against my hand. Through the darkness of my almost unconscious senses came an alien pain – a stab such as many badly wounded people feel under deep narcosis when the surgeon's saw starts its work. My fingers worked automatically and grabbed the joystick.

"Hold tight, pilot. It was high time."

The threatening jolting of the metal column slowly had an effect on my firmly closed hand; life returned to my numbed arm and woke me from my icy coma.

My trembling left hand wiped away the red smear from my eyes and the painful, urgent groan rose to a wild scream. Terror opened my eyes wide and a wild will to live was born. In a mad whirl the earth rotated and danced in red and green patches in front of my tortured face.

Take it quietly... gain time... I acted as though hypnotized – acted instinctively in the way foreseen in theory for such eventualities and repeatedly taught in flying schools.

I was spinning to the left, so I must apply full right rudder; but, for heaven's sake, I was using full throttle... Pull the lever back quickly. Opposite rudder... keep her there. The right foot stretched full home on the rudder bar... more... The whole leg stretched until it could go no further. Stick central... a short burst of throttle. Now take it easy....

That was all I could do.

The brightly-coloured disc began to rotate more slowly and the ground grew more distinct in detail. Now in the whirling dance I could already pick out farms, moors, canals.... Those villages and towns below were no longer the size of matchboxes as they had appeared at 21,000 feet. The landscape below seemed to be terrifyingly large as it turned. Take it easy... even if the earth seems to be drawing dangerously close. Keep your wits about you... If you get out of one spin too quickly, you will begin to spin in the opposite direction. The slipstream is not yet bringing full pressure to bear on the rudder but another spin now means the end of everything.

The rotating ground below stood still. Slowly the controls began to answer in my hands. Now I could use my rudder....

I'm saved, I thought excitedly. For the first time I again felt the rapid beating of my heart and my chest grew hot and congested.

So now pull her out very slowly....

More yet... The steep landscape started to move and the approaching earth streaked ever faster below the Focke. Now I had to use both hands and all my strength to pull the stick right back into my stomach. At incredible speed the earth grew larger; like threatening devils' masks, the grotesque shapes of factory chimneys appeared in front of my windscreen. With my last ounce of strength I pulled on the stick. Two trembling fists of steel clutched the cold metal. My body ached as it was pressed into the seat. All the blood rushed into my legs and brought a sense of lameness, as though they had been blown up by an invisible pump.

My heart...

My lips were torn open and my jaw fell limply on my chest. A dull hissing and singing in my ears... Soft veils bringing a numbing wave of black and violet spots before the eyes. The force of my hands threatened to make me unconscious once more....

Instinctively I knew that I had got her under control, and while the Focke sped over a hedge my glazed eyes glanced at the air-speed indicator. God in heaven! The needle was standing at the limit, nearly 600 miles an hour.

Good old trusty Focke. All those aircraft experts who talked of the danger of reaching and exceeding the sound barrier, and argued about the difficulties of designing fighters for use at such speeds... and you, you good old girl, were safe and sound, your wings had not collapsed and your rudder was not broken with the incredible pressure...

The iron vice round my aching forehead seemed to relax. The over-exerted heart once more pumped the red blood into my emptied brain.

"I'm safe," I cried to myself. And then I was aware of the blood which was still running down my face. Christ, the cabin was like a sieve.

Ah yes, of course. At 21,000 there had been that bitter scrap with the Thunderbolts. Those blasted "crates" had never been seen before at such a height and it was a long time since things had been so hot.

I must have been hit. From the cabin things looked all right but I had been lucky. At least the Yank had not damaged my machine.

But what about my "winger", *Oberleutnant* Heinz Seiffert? The former bomber pilot who had won his Knight's Cross over England. He was the only one who had been with me at the time.

I now felt unbearably weary. The strain of the last few minutes had been too much for me.

I must be playing the goat somewhere over the Ems, I decided, trying to find my bearings. That must have been Meppen... or Lingen.

So if I turn south-east I'll come to a river, the Hase... or a canal, our old friend the Mitteland Canal.

A right-hand turn...

Hell, what was that? Bloody fool! You've just hit a hightension cable. A proper mess-up. The Focke gave a jolt and I had to put on full left rudder.

A huge piece had been ripped off the right wing-tip.

I was now wide awake once more. I cursed bitterly at my momentary weakness which had now taken a terrible revenge. And then, to make matters worse, the engine began to run unevenly, coughing and spluttering.

Now what was the matter? The "eternal light" was flickering. No more gas.... Get down as fast as possible before the engine conks completely. A short zoom and a quick look round. Yes, there was a broad, empty strip of meadow.

I opened the cabin roof. (In a crash-landing it can become jammed and it would not be the first time that a pilot had been burnt to death because he could no longer open his cockpit.)

Slowly I put Yellow 6 down on the marshy grass.

"I'm sorry, old 'crate'. You saved my life and this is my thanks. You were the best one I ever flew..."

I thoughtfully stroked the left wing as if I were taking leave of it, stroked the scratched plates which bore the scars of fifty air battles.

The first peasants came running up to help me as I leaned over the cockpit of my favourite aircraft, taking out the parachute, the maps and the ignition key as a souvenir.

A "*Grünherz*" car fetched me from Lingen. I was surprised to see *Hauptmann* Funk and Neumann, the Adjutant, sitting in the back seat.

"This is indeed an honour," I said. "What brings you here?"

"Hmm, Heilmann, we thought things might be worse," replied Neumann, taking me gently by the arm and settling me comfortably in the front seat of the Hansa.

"You see, Willi," Funk said in a serious voice, "the rest of the boys landed a long time ago with the exception of Seiffert and yourself. We were just about to call up the neighbouring airfields to see if anyone had landed there when Seiffert called on his radio and, in a great state of excitement, informed us that you'd been shot down by four Thunderbolts on your tail."

"That's right," said the Adjutant, breaking in. "And then a terrible groan came on the headphones and we had no more contact with him."

I knew at once.

"Did you find him?"

"Yes. He's had it..." Funk said after an embarrassed pause. "Naturally at siesta time after lunch I couldn't find anybody to come along. Heinz must have baled out near the ground. He lay a few hundred yards away from his burntout machine. It was terrible. He was crouching there, the parachute was half open and both his legs were well stuck in the bog, with his back in a small hole which he himself had made from his impact. His head had fallen backwards and the white silk canopy seemed to have spread over him like a shroud.

"Heinz must have broken his neck... he looked so natural in the posture. His Knight's Cross hung down in its right position. "

"Poor devil," I said in a hoarse voice and thought that my two comrades might quite easily be saying the same thing about myself had I not tweaked the nose of death at the very last moment.

Then I remembered the wife, that cheerful, serene, fairhaired girl from Dresden – Heinz Seiffert's wife. She had been spending the last fortnight with her husband. Many of the pilots let their wives come and visit them at the station because they were homeless now that the Red tide was sweeping over the Eastern Front.

"Now you see, Walter, how right I was when I said only last night in the mess that our wives here must be absolutely scared to death and that it will destroy them. A woman doesn't belong in our circle... apart from the few tarts we find to pass the time away – but one's wife, the great love...?"

"No. None of them can stand it."

Two hours later I stood, with a white bandage round my head, in front of this woman, trying painfully to find the words to tell her what had happened. But I had no need of words because she obviously knew already. Such a tortured face, as white as a ghost, and those sympathetic, reproachful eyes could only bring a message of death...

I put my arms round her, and as she began to weep, I laid her fair-haired head on my chest. I could not help thinking sadly of my own wife and hoped desperately that she would be spared what I had to impart almost daily so roughly and brutally in a last letter to those who remained behind.

* * *

After a mere week's rest, my superficial wound was healed. Day after day now I flew two or three missions.

The distress of the German fighter arm became unbearable.

The machines lost were very soon replaced; the heavy industries worked magnificently, pouring more and more aircraft onto the airfields than there were pilots to fly them.

It read like a fairy tale when one learnt that, despite nonstop round-the-clock bombing attacks, nearly 40,000 aircraft had left the German works during the past year. This was almost double the figure for the year 1942 when the Flying Fortresses had first begun their area bombing – in March

1942 Lübeck and Rostock, followed up by an attack on Cologne, where in one night alone there were 10,000 dead.

Nevertheless, it must be repeated that although German industry was still working, and working well, there was a sorry lack of pilots and *Staffelkapitaen*. The pilots who could fly these machines against the enemy grew ever smaller in numbers...

* * *

I was in despair. Two hundred of the ground staff had been taken from my *Gruppe* and replaced by women... It was absolutely crazy to try and replace skilled men with more or less empty-headed girls. I dared not say anything against the zeal of the German women in the aircraft factories and workshops, but it was absolutely ridiculous for them to be on a service station. Conditions there were very different from what those behind the lines probably envisaged.

Quite apart from the fact that these women were obviously the scrapings of the pot. From Hamburg, Berlin, Frankfurt and goodness knows where else, these last reserves of women had been bundled together without intelligence or consideration. Courageous soldiers'wives with no children, young typists from non-essential businesses, and whores from the big city brothels...

So this was how they expected to win a war.

Our manpower was to be injected with women in order to build up an army capable of taking the offensive. And this was to be done in three weeks.

And now the women were to fill up the gaps. The whole routine of missions must suffer if the hard-working technical staff was taken away. This was too obvious to comment upon.

When my *Staffelkapitaen* and I went into the orderly room it was no longer the usual atmosphere of sweating soldiers, leather and tobacco that met our nostrils but an enchanting odour of perfume. We could hardly believe our eyes... One fine day behind the women's barracks charming crepe-de-chine cami-knicks and lace-edged panties were hanging on a clothes-line.

I had never thought that one day I would have to issue an order forbidding women's pink underclothes made of blackmarket parachute silk to be hung in view of the airmen for fear it should take their minds off their work.

But this dangerous operation of using "fighter dolls" on the station, thanks to the strict discipline enforced by everyone, from the *Kommandeur* down to the *Oberfeldwebel*, worked better than was to have been imagined. The feminine infiltration we had feared so much was finally digested.

This, however, did not prevent my leading mechanic, instead of working on his aircraft, disappearing with his female mate into the nearby fields, leaving their footprints on the springy moss and between the young spring green of the pines. When the *Feldwebel*'s voice rang out, angrily calling their names, two very red-faced youngsters with feigned innocence stumbled out of the undergrowth where for a few moments... they had been looking for a cloth to polish the machine.

There were, of course, hyenas among these girls. Thus two pilots from a nearby fighter wing plunged to their deaths because their parachutes had not unfolded. In actual fact they never could have opened because they were not there in the green pack. For a long time the canopies had served as underclothes for these utterly heartless females whose greed for silk did not bilk at murdering German pilots.

"Yes," said Kurt Knebe, on one occasion when these unbearable conditions were being discussed. " We've gone back a few hundred years in history. The *Gefreiters* will become *Gefreiter*-ettes and we shall have *vivandières* following the soldiers. All that's missing now is the old brothel mother carrying an Amazon flag and our modern mercenaries will be quite in order."

"But don't forget that the greater part of our girls are poor little things who remain clean and respectable and have never been kissed," replied Patt.

"And in their anxiety and trouble are thinking of their men on active service..."

"Yes, you've forgotten them," laughed Prager. "But it doesn't matter, you know. They're all human beings and a few professional whores create the same effect as a handful of drunken soldiers in a low dive. The public only notice them while the majority of the respectable and the modest carry on quite unobserved."

Chapter Seventeen

THE DAYS passed swiftly...

The pilots knew every inch of the country between the Weser and the Rhine; the Teutoburger Wald, the Sauerland, the Eifel, the vivid green Munster basin as far as the ruined cities of the Ruhr. Each day brought new missions, new air battles and new losses...

The Hurtgenwald south of Aachen became a terrible graveyard. It changed hands a score of times and then the German front collapsed in the face of superior odds.

Again and again the fighters were chased into the air from their sectors between Lingen and Vechta, Kloppenburg and the Mitteland Canal... through the barrage erected against enemy penetration into the Ruhr, to give support to the front line. It no longer lay in their power to do this with any visible effect owing to the fact that go per cent of all the air battles took place over the Munster basin.

In nearly every large village, behind age-old, grey, weatherbeaten cemetery walls, lay the graves of fallen "*Grünherz*" pilots.

* * *

Dortenmann was posted away with twenty-five Fockes. He now took off from Babenhausen, between Darmstadt and Aschaffenburg, and reported successes in scraps with the fighter-bombers in the Rhine-Main sector. I hoped that the whole fighter wing would be transferred there. It was my own home and in such grim times of war one likes to be as near to home as possible.

But this hope was not realised. After a fortnight Dortenmann was back in Varrelbusch. Surprisingly enough, he had been very successful, but the cost had been very heavy. A quarter of his pilots had paid with their lives in tough air battles with Thunderbolts over the Taunus area.

"Did you pay my respects to the old country, Hans?" I said with a laugh as I greeted the wanderers.

"You bet we did, you old buzzard," and then the slim, sinewy Würzburger gave his report.

"I just can't understand," he said, "why they didn't send you all after me and why I've got to come back here. It was much easier going back there, and above all the front was nearer and we didn't have to fly so far to get to it, but now I'm also beginning to realise that among those cretins there isn't a brain left that hasn't gone completely addled."

"Who's that over there?" asked Dortenmann as a certain *Hauptmann* Tapper, who had just been posted to the *Gruppe*, entered the mess.

"You'd better watch your step, Hans. That's the stoolpigeon who's been sent to spy on us cowardly fighter pilots."

With a smile I introduced the two men.

"*Leutnant* Dortenmann, *Staffelkapitän* of *Staffel* 10, and this, Hans, is *Hauptmann* Tapper, our NSFO."[1]

Nobody took kindly to being spied upon by these gentlemen who crept around in carpet slippers and, with antiquated Nazi slogans, tried to influence the conduct of the staffel. They were always known as the "Arse-crawling Brigade".

We all loathed these Commissar types and considered their presence among us to be an insult. Tapper was therefore kept completely outside our circle and every time he appeared the conversation suddenly ceased or changed completely.

⋆ ⋆ ⋆

"*Autobahn!* Are we clear to proceed, please?"

The *Gruppe* was flying southwards at 12,000 feet over the crest of the Teutoburger Wald. Between thick banks of cloud we could occasionally see small sections of the country below. The Fockes flew through the mighty, mountainous source of a high layer of cumulus.

"From *Autobahn*. Your sector is free of enemy aircraft. Fourengined formations are on their way from Southern Holland."

A slight change of course to 250°. I decided to make a bee-line for Aachen-Duisburg.

The huge banks of cloud towered in heavy layers. Cut off smooth below at 6,000 feet, as if they had been placed on a gigantic glass plate, they looked like wobbly jellies.

We were soon over Münster. Once more we plunged into a milky wall through which we caught an occasional glimpse of the city below that kept disappearing like a ghost.

"Flat out, boys. Boeings overhead," shouted an excited voice over the intercom. A hasty glance aloft. It was enough to make the blood freeze in our veins. Scarcely a hundred feet above us, comingin fromstarboard, Boeings were flyingwing tip to wing tip. The open bomb bays yawned like black jaws.

"That lot's destined for Münster. They're going to drop their bombs at any moment."

[1] Nationalsozialistischer Führungsoffizier. Corresponds to a political commissar.

"Let them lay their eggs." That was the irrepressible Prager, shooting off his mouth, keeping his nerve even in this dire moment. He must have steel cords where other people have thin white nerves, I thought.

The bombs hissed past.

Tumbling and whistling downwards, bombs, bombs, bombs... We could clearly recognise each one of these murderous objects as they left the bays.

Holding their breath in icy impatience, the sixty pilots clutched their control columns. Grim tortured faces... hands on the red buttons to eject the cabins, although there was no salvation if one of those bombs hit them.

Anything rather than look at those open holds vomiting their deadly venom. These were no eggs, as they used to say in fighter circles... It was an insatiable cloudburst, releasing a sickly wobbling fish spawn.

At last we were through the hail.

None of us had been hit. It was barely credible!

"Ugh" came an occasional groan of relief, and one could almost hear the beating of hearts in the intercom.

"Heilmann to *Autobahn*. Why the hell didn't you bloody cretins report the bombers that we've nearly rammed?"

"*Autobahn* to Heilmann. We weren't notified."

"You weren't notified." I mocked the voice coming over the intercom. "Well, I hope nothing will be notified when one of you falls on his bloody arse."

And then: "Permission to attack, please. I'll wait for it..."

"*Autobahn* to Heilmann. You are to carry out your front-line mission."

"Don't be such a bloody clod. We shall never get another chance at the Boeings in the clouds."

"*Autobahn* to Heilmann. Fly to your target as ordered."

"I hope you live to regret this, you bloody twat."

* * *

I had hardly landed before I was ordered to report to *General* Wolf. I was given a shattering rocket. I would never have given the *General* credit for such a torrent of abuse although he was known for his energy and forceful bearing. No, I would never have believed that he could have been so vulgar...

"All my respects for your flow of language, my dear boy, but if it's ever repeated I'll haul you up before a court martial."

"*Jawohl, Herr General.*" (This with outstretched hand that nearly hit the infuriated *General* in the face, and swearing under my breath.)

"What do you know of front-line needs? Suppose a mass attack had been planned and five minutes before zero hour the Luftwaffe was prevented from launching it because, in an attempt to shoot down a few bombers, you hadn't turned up."

"*Jawohl, Herr General.*" (My brain turned to ice. Here was one of these bloody parade-ground stallions who, despite all his "climbing", had no brains left talking about a mass attack by the fighter arm with sixty fighters and referring to hundreds of Boeings as a few bombers!)

Then the *General* offered me a genuine dark Havana – a treat after all the ersatz cigars we had been smoking. We had quite a pleasant conversation in a cloud of blue smoke over a glass of brandy. This "brass hat" did not seem to be a bad fellow. Service is service, and brandy is brandy and the rather one-sided conversation took place quite cosily.

"You're the first man," said the *General*, "during my whole military career who has ever made such a remark to me. Tell me, what actually is a twat?"

"You must excuse me, *General*. It's an expression we use in Rheinhesse. It means the same thing as an oaf in Cologne, a nitwit in Munich, or in ordinary conversation – if you'll excuse me, *General* – a bloody idiot."

"Umh. I must say it's very, very flattering."

"I apologise sincerely, *General*. I had no idea that you were on the phone in person." (I very nearly said "in the front line".)

"All right, young man; but a different tone next time, please."

⋆ ⋆ ⋆

A few days later the same type of incident occurred.

Once more our mission was against the front line. Once more the clouds were favourable – rather more gaps in them this time – and once more *Autobahn* reported the sector free from enemy aircraft.

And once more it was over Münster.

This time the "*Grünherz*" came out of the clouds above the Boeings which were flying in, wave after wave.

"Heilmann to *Autobahn*. Heavy 'buses' over Münster. Am engaged in a dog-fight."

This time I used my brain. I merely reported that I had gone into the attack. I had to jettison my auxiliary tank and Aachen had had it for the day.

"Heilmann to all pilots. We're going in."

I dared not give any precise attacking orders lest the people on the ground should understand and threaten me with a court martial as on the previous occasion.

A gradual sweep to starboard so as to attack from headon, which is the best position against four-engined bombers. Cutting through the lower formations, the inside machines took up their place next to me, while those who had previously been to port of my machine, gaining altitude, carried out a perfect 90° turn. This re-grouping had to take place in a wide sweep and each machine had to make an absolutely identical turn.

The range was 400 yards...

"Attack from above..."

300 yards...

The Boeings appeared like barn doors in the sights.

"Fire!" The tracers were pumped ruthlessly into their thick bellies. The Yanks did not take things lying down, and while the pilots obstinately held their course a hail of lead from a dozen cannon spurted from each Boeing against the attackers. The cannon fired through the propeller blades replied, and four heavy machine-guns hacked pieces out of the big bombers. Plates flew off, smoke poured from the engines and fires broke out.

The American aircraft had magnificent fire-extinguishing apparatus on board. Smaller fires were put out easily, particularly in the engines. The fuel tanks were protected with india rubber which was self-sealing when a bullet pierced it. It had to be a direct hit to set one of these "crates" on fire and to bring it down.

Away to my right a Boeing exploded in the air.

So far they had not jettisoned their bombs.

Two more Boeings were caught up in the explosion and white parachutes could be seen blossoming in the sky.

At last the harassed bomber stream jettisoned their bombs. Even had they done nothing else, the fighters could consider their attack a success.

A gigantic shadow loomed up in front of my windscreen. I pressed the firing button and fired with all I had got. I pumped my bullets into the Perspex windscreen in front of the pilot's seat.

Then I yanked the Focke away to the left, streaked below the following Boeing and dived down out of range of the American's fire.

"Re-group in a left-hand circle. We're going in for a second attack."

A good half of the *Gruppe* rejoined their *Gruppen Kommandeur*'s machine with its red painted tail unit.

"Heilmann from Cromm. Mustangs below. Same number as ourselves."

"Where?"

"Right below the bombers. 3,000 feet lower flying in the same direction."

"Victor."

Then we waded in to attack the second stream at a close angle from below. Once more huge shadows firing desperately appeared in the cross-wires. "Full gas, supercharger..." Increased revs gave increased firing speed.

Ruthlessly and without wavering we approached the enemy through the murderous defence fire. How wonderful it would have been now had we possessed double the speed of the jets for our attack.

"Fire!" More blazing machines and parachutes... Small flashes ran along my right wing. A hit. Hell, it couldn't matter less. Press on, fire.

Blazing furiously, the heavy machine tottered in my sights, remained vertical for a moment, then fell over on its right wing and dived steeply.

The stocky Bavarian *Gefreiter* Sens reported a damaged engine. I could hear him cursing over the intercom. He must have had a direct hit. This was not surprising, for the gunners in the Boeings were also fighting for their lives.

Then we made our way through the formation again. Climbing turn...

"Cromm. Where are you?"

"I've broken off the action. They kept coming... I'm already over Teuto."

"Victor. We're coming after you."

The last aircraft dived at nearly 400 mph away from the battlefield. We flitted over the crest of the Teutoburger Wald that lay before us like a wall.

That evening we learned that the remains of twenty-four heavy bombers lay scattered over the countryside; but most important of all, the whole bomber stream of some two hundred machines had jettisoned its bombs just outside Münster in open country. It had cost us twelve of our comrades, but against this the lives of thousands of men, women and children had been saved. This mission had really been worth while.

Once more bitter fighting broke out in the Aachen sector on the German frontier. It seemed as though the enemy were making an all-out attempt in his last offensive.

Pidder Cromm was sitting in his room, listening to the Forces Radio West news from his home town. The others had gone to the mess to see a new film. Every evening a new film was shown to distract the men's attention.

But Pidder Cromm did not feel like going to the pictures. At home the Tommies might show up at any moment. He could not help thinking of his parents... small frail people.

I threw myself down on my camp bed fully dressed. My cigarette had no taste. I jumped up with nerves on edge, went into the corridor and knocked up Prager and Cromm. Would they like a game of skat in my room? I had brought a bottle of Hennessy out of my cupboard.

The jazz music broke off. "This is the Forces programme Radio West. We are giving you the latest news from the front line."

None of us gave it a thought that we were disobeying Goebbels' strict orders at the risk of hard labour, concentration camp or penal battalion – the infamous penal battalions 500 or 999 from which there was no escape. We all listened to the enemy broadcasts. Combined with our own Wehrmacht communique a clear-headed person could get a true picture of the position. Above all, the BBC broadcasts gave us news of missing comrades. Thus day by day for over a week we had heard a long list of pilots who had remained on the other side after the successful though disastrous New Year's attack.

"Keep quiet," said Pidder, nervously waving his hand although no one had spoken a word. Conditions in the Aachen sector were just coming through. Things were still chaotic, so the British had not yet captured the town.

"It may last for some time, Pidder."

"You may be right, Heilmann, but things can't go on like this."

"Switch the bloody thing off. What follows is only rubbish," mumbled Prager angrily. Blowing the smoke of his cigarette through his nostrils, he asked me: "When are these new orders coming along that they keep talking about? I mean that the west part of the Rhine is to be evacuated and all that?"

"Yes. We keep on retreating until the day we shall have to stick up our hands."

There was a knock on the door.

"Come in."

It was Kurt Knebe. A slightly embarrassed smile appeared on his burnt face.

"Well, Kurt, without your Gusti?" joked Prager.

"What do you know, old fellow? She's waiting over at my place and that's why I've looked you up. I was to give you her kind regards and we want to be alone, you understand? So don't disturb us, will you?"

"All right, you old night-fighter. Enjoy yourself."

Knebe left the room with a laugh.

I poured out the brandy. "Good luck, boys."

"*Prosit*."

Prager cleared his throat. "I don't know why these connoisseurs think so much of French brandy. It's far too soapy for my taste. Ugh!"

Cromm shuffled the cards. They were cut and he dealt.

But our minds were not really on the game. I pursued the conversation which Knebe had interrupted.

"There's a buzz going round about bombs the size of an apple," I said.

"Do you still believe in the fairy tale of the seven-league boots? I'm not that stupid," said Prager angrily. "Give me the cards. There's been enough talk of death and destruction."

"Take it easy, Heini," said Pidder Cromm. "When the 'scrambled eggs' start whispering something, there's no smoke without fire. That's our bad luck. One thing is certain: these bombs were discussed at the last gauleiter meeting. The Kloppenburger section leader went into a huddle yesterday with Tapper and mentioned that he had already seen the blueprints."

"Well, that's the tragedy of Germany today: Men. Every clown becomes a smaller or larger Reich defence commissar and we, who are really concerned, only hear a lot of bull about miracle weapons from those nattering sparrows. It's a surprise to me that all the children don't know what's going on in Peenemünde."

"Peenemünde? Is that a branch of the Kummersdorf research station?"

"No, boys. Something quite different," I said. "Kummersdorf and Rehagen are the home of arms test station *Staffel* 5. In 1939 I met there the girl who is now my wife. After her unit was transferred to Von Braun in Peenemünde, I married her in February 1940 to get her out of that powder closet. I can tell you one thing and you can believe me or not as you please: even today my wife would not breathe the slightest word that might contravene her secrecy oath. I know a lot, but what these Party boys, intentionally exploiting the credulity of the masses, blare forth to the world in general is nothing less than high treason."

"But we still don't know what's being cooked up in Peenemünde," insisted Prager.

"Oh, that's quite simple. 'V' weapons, rocket research... it's all tied up with this mysterious bomb."

"I won't prang my own hometown," said Pidder Cromm with compressed lips, "even if I have to mutiny at the last moment."

"Don't worry too much about it, Pidder," I said, trying to calm him down. "I think it's far too late to use this weapon on our own country even if it actually exists."

"Well, what's the good of discussing it all? Let's get on with the game. We at least know exactly where we are."

Keeping up a running commentary, Prager dealt the cards. The night dragged on...

Chapter Eighteen

February 2nd, 1945

SPRING arrived very early that year. The warm sun had melted the last snows, the warm clothes of the past weeks J had been discarded and the pilots, in polo shirts and shorts, sunbathed in deck chairs. A few of them were already starting to get sunburnt. Light, air and sun brought back some health into their pallid bodies.

A peaceful atmosphere reigned in the *Gruppe*.

At dawn the "*Grünherz* choir" spent a cheerful quarter of an hour and invited me to an early-morning drink since it was my birthday. The pilots wished me "many happy returns" and the ground staff joined in. I was carried on their shoulders three times round the mess. Good luck and many more Tallyho's! Tapper wished me "Good luck, strength and a faithful heart in Germany's bitterest hour".

A birthday is sacred to superstitious pilots. To fly on such a day is blasphemy.

So that day I did not take off. I took my walking stick, which I had carved and decorated in my spare time, and went for a walk through the pine woods. I wanted to be alone with my thoughts. A few hours' relaxation was splendid for over-taxed nerves. I breathed the warm spicy air of the pines into my lungs.

The moles were already at work. Fresh hills of black peat rose on either side of the forest path. It pleased me to think of these little grey creatures with their pale pink noses, to think that they had just awakened from their winter sleep.

The noise of aircraft engines droned from the airfield some distance away. The whine of engines told me that a mission was under way. A few moments later I could see slim fuselages in the morning sun. Yellow, red, black and white numbered Fockes took off, grouped and then flew off in formation in a southerly direction.

Good luck, boys, and good hunting, I thought, waving my stick.

However, I broke my resolution when, that evening just before the end of ops time, we were ordered to take off again, on a free-for-all chase of Mustangs and Thunderbolts in the neighbourhood.

It had been hot all day and the blue sky seemed generous in its warmth. The *Gruppe* had flown many hours and had suffered all manner of vicissitudes. Knebe had force-landed and Prager had a slight shrapnel wound.

So I climbed into my Yellow 6. Everything in flying superstition spoke against my flying.

As the "*Grünherz*" took off they were attacked over the airfield. The first Fockes spun down like burning torches out of the sky just as *Staffel* 9 was taking off.

I flew low over headquarters and made off to the north but I was alone, for my *Staffel* had been late in following my dive. Patt had made the mistake and zoomed too high with his machine. The others followed him, thinking that my aircraft was still in front. Patt led them right into the scrap below and they had to fight for their lives.

I joined the party. I was furious, for my plan to change places with the rear squadron so as to gain height and bring help from above had now come to grief. This could cost us a lot of useful blood. A flight of machines diving in from above could have changed matters, but now...

I climbed at twenty feet per second. I would see if there was anything left to rescue. Perhaps I could shoot down one or two of the enemy machines as a last resort.

But soon I was spotted and attacked. No, that's too much, I thought, as I recognised five Mustangs bearing down on me.

Stall turn. Full gas and break off the action...

The Mustangs' guns spat savagely behind me, pursuing the Focke down to the ground. But I was faster, and in the mad chase over the hedges I shook off my pursuers.

Everything was flat and green. The compass pointed to the north. Good God! Ahead lay water. Hell, they've chased me as far as the sea! That must be the "drink".

I zoomed cautiously to get my bearings. A left-hand bank over the broad expanse of water. Land suddenly appeared below my wings. An airfield in the distance...

Better go down. I'd be able to find out from the ground boys what was cooking at Varrelbusch and take off again. A gentle turn, undercarriage lowered...

A fantastic firework display greeted my landing Focke.

Naturally, you cretins. How could I expect anything else. A mission ruined... jittery ack-ack gunners expecting Mustangs... And my birthday to cap it all.

I fired my red flares, but not until I was right over the field and just about to touch down did the rain of fire suddenly cease.

"Well, I suppose I had to expect that," I muttered under my breath as I got out of the machine.

"Leave the aircraft here. I'm taking off again at once," I shouted to the ground crew who rushed up. Then I gave a rocket to the gunnery officer, advising him to show his men the aircraft recognition charts which were displayed in the hangars.

At station headquarters I received the necessary information about air conditions in the Varrelbusch sector. Fighter-bombers were still cruising about in the neighbourhood. I had better wait a bit. I was near an estuary on a combined sea and land airfield.

A *Hauptmann* with light-red collar badges came up. He had a bottle in his hand. "I'm very sorry, old chap," he said sympathetically.

"Oh, don't you worry, *Hauptmann*. It's happened to me before and it will probably happen again, only it's my birthday today and despite the brilliance of the fireworks it wasn't very pleasant to be wished a happy birthday in that way."

With a smile we shook hands.

"Well, let me wish you one now. I can't think of any better use that my Veuve Clicquot could be put to."

In the late twilight, when the All Clear had come through from Varrelbusch, I landed my Yellow 6.

⋆ ⋆ ⋆

When I entered the mess I found that a magnificent trans. formation had taken place. It looked like a scene from the *Arabian Nights*. Three parachutes had been hung from the ceiling and a blue light shone from above upon the silk canopies.

"Where did you blighters get the stars from?" I asked with delight.

"Pinz conjured them up from somewhere, sir, with cardboard and scissors," replied Patt with a grin. His freckled face shone like a full moon on a spring night.

A magnificent evening began.

To eat there was roast pork which had been brought from Hesepe, followed by exquisite pastries and coffee; and much later, about four o'clock in the morning, we sat round like conspirators on real Oriental divans with blankets and cushions we had managed to scrounge. A host of "dead men" showed that it had been a very tough drinking bout.

Now we were drinking black coffee once more to cool our thick heads.

Dortenmann, after a long philosophical observation of the artificial starry sky, suddenly remarked that there was no moon. He clambered up on to the flat hut roof vociferously maintaining that he would certainly haul the moon down from heaven.

"Bring... lemons, Mischo, and s... ugar and schn... apps," I ordered, stuttering weakly.

"Schnapps is all right, Chief, but lemon juice..."

"Keep quiet, Patt, you bloody fool. You don't understand anything. I'm going to mix a cocktail."

"Rubbish. Haven't you ever heard of a Nikolaschka?"

Mischo, the orderly, put the required ingredients on a small table, but before my trembling hands could arrange the glasses and prepare the drink Muller-Berber, Patt, Prager and Sandelmeyer had used the sugar in their coffee.

I sent for some more sugar and asked for some more coffee for myself.

But again there was a setback. The drunken pilots blew the coffee grains into each other's faces. The lemon fell to the floor and immediately an exciting football match was in progress. The yellow fruit was soon squashed and rolled under a stool.

Pidder Cromm crawled about on all fours on the ground shouting "Where the hell's the ball? Who's done away with the ball?"

Mischo brought more ingredients and after a great struggle the cocktail was ready – and did it taste good! Glasses were held out for more and more rounds. A squeeze of lemon, a teaspoonful of sugar added, which now had a brown crust of ground coffee. We gobbled up the schnapps, sucked the lemon. Soon there was none left. While an accordion player brought to an end his sentimental tango *Little Anushka*, Knebe, staring at his glass, began to sing *Sweet Little Nikolaschka*.

At this moment Dortenmann rushed into the mess in a great state of excitement. We must all come outside. He'd caught the moon. He'd shot it clean out of the sky.

The whole mess rushed out yelling and laughing into the open air. A bright starry sky lay above us in all its glittering majesty and the fresh night wind cooled our hot foreheads. And there was the moon in its last quarter.

Hans Dortenmann explained how he had built it. Now amidst a great uproar began the complicated task of catching it. Dortenmann had dismantled one of the kitchen-stove pipes and was now pointing it at the moon. Patt, holding the pipe, was wobbling dangerously to and fro on a rickety stool. On Dortenmann's instructions he had to keep his hands in front of the opening when the moon came into view in the pipe.

From time to time Patt gave a thunderous bang on the pipe with his huge paws and a cloud of soot fell on Dortenmann's face at the other end. He kept on belching and crying: "It's gone and yet I had it absolutely in the cross-wires." The game began again.

What a night! How magnificent to relax among your pals, comrades of the air, comrades of death and comrades of your everyday life.

We kept up our skylarking and the mood was very high, thanks to the alcohol we had drunk. In this state of excitement, our nerves were put at their ease for one night – "put on ice" as Patt said.

Now the twitter of birds waking up with the dawn occasionally mingled with the strains of the accordion. A dreamy passage from a song nostalgically recalling the red lamps of San Pauli was interrupted by a few trills which passed unheeded by the singers.

A banging of doors, a bustle in the corridor, along which people were being carried to bed and that was the end... Peace slowly returned to this airfield among the woods and the men slept on into a new day.

⋆ ⋆ ⋆

Cologne

The gay home of the Rhinelanders, the city of Gothic spires. The black filigree of the cathedral towers still pointed skywards. Small and insignificant, the old part of the city lay broken and crushed among the ruins. At one time beautiful mediaeval buildings with pointed gables had clustered round the cathedral square. The sprawling Gürzenich square...

Poor Cologne. You too have lost your plumage. You were more beautiful ten years ago, I thought, remembering a gay carnival which I had once witnessed there.

Cologne, like all the cities on the Rhine, was now a heap of smoking ruins. The four-engined bombers had completed their gruesome task and now twin-engined Marauders and fighter-bombers were ravaging the last remains and keeping the population in a state of nerves. The "*Grünherz*" circled overhead trying to defend the city.

Yes, Cologne must fall any day. Ruthlessly the war hastened to its close, hastened towards collapse.

Aachen... Düren... and now Cologne.

The whole of the bank left on the Rhine north of Bonn was in enemy hands. Like insatiable, Cyclopean caterpillars the Shermans and Churchills devoured our burning homeland. Long columns of motorised infantry followed in their wake like greedy centipedes.

Despite the courageous defence of the German divisions there was no halting them. Strategy was inefficient, supplies could not be brought up and there were no more reserves and ammunition.

Then came the strategic withdrawals, as the Wehrmacht High Command now expressed it in their own language – a kind of self-justification which deceived no one.

When a break-through was halted at great cost three other gaps were torn in the front line. This lagging resistance had become a military paralysis and the final collapse was only a question of time. Within four weeks there would be nothing left to defend. In those days the tactical advantage of the inner line became the subject of a cynical joke, for, each time the High Command gave up a few miles, a thousand more bombs fell into the mousetrap.

Day after day the "*Grünherz*" took off. Our flights were now quite short, although to us the dog-fights seemed endless.

Cologne... Bonn... Duisburg... Wesel...

The old Münster witch's cauldron, from Essen to Paderborn and along the Teuto to Rheine – the "Happy Valley", as the enemy fighters called this crucial sector.

At a great height – this was now the only security for fighters – sixty Fockes circled over the bend in the Weser near Minden. Visibility was poor. The thick cumulus clouds left gaps through which small areas of the ground could be seen. It was a magnificent sight. The thick bales of cumulus sped by, if driven by a shepherd, below the cirrus which lay like a transparent veil in the gleaming blue.

The vertical rays of the afternoon sun produced a fairy landscape of enchanted shadowy outlines, the dark and bright contours of which, tinged with tender blue, deep green and violet delighted our eyes.

I handed over the leadership to Dortenmann and went down a few thousand feet with my staffel in order to keep a better watch. We were looking for fighter-bombers over Osnabruck; five different formations of them had been reported.

The shallow valley of the Else, which flows through Werra into the Weser, lay below us as we set a westerly course. Then the river veered away to the west; a few hundred yards farther on the Hase emerged from the Teutoburger Wald feeling its way westwards to the Ems.

Six thousand feet below us a few dozen Thunderbolts were cruising. Pidder Cromm had spotted them and now reported them over the intercom.

"From Heilmann. Come on down, Dortenmann. I'll stay above you."

Forty Fockes dived through the gaps in the clouds like greedy hawks.

Flight after flight swooped down onto the enemy. Hoarse cries of excitement rang out over the intercom. Only about once a year did we ever have an opportunity like this of attacking from above out of thick cloud.

How wonderful flying must be for the Allies who usually won all their air victories in these conditions.

But this time they had to fight for their lives.

The first attack brought down five Thunderbolts. The enemy broke up into a chaotic jumble. The Yankees were trying desperately to break away. Pidder Cromm attacked with his black Focke. Two parachutes unfolded. One of the Thunderbolts flicked onto its back and then dived in a crazy loop ever faster and steeper towards the earth. A long burst of flame hissed through the afternoon sky and then ballooned into a black column of smoke above the glowing red.

Prager dived like an arrow with his white machine on a formation of twelve Mustangs which had rushed up to help.

I remained, icy cold, watching for an opportunity to take my part in this dog-fight. It was wonderful to see how the three *Staffelkapitaen* forced the enemy further and further to the ground. If the Americans could not shake them off it would mean the end of them.

Now the Mustangs were trying to get away but I had already begun my attack on them. Three crashed in flames. The remainder broke off the engagement and were driven into the crazy network of fighting aircraft, into the scarlet necklaces of tracer bullets zig-zagging like fairy needles across the sky.

I again took up my position with *Staffel* 9. None of my aircraft seemed to be missing but about twenty fires were burning on the ground below.

"From Heilmann. Speed it up, boys. We must be getting low in juice."

"Knebe to Heilmann. Have a look behind you to starboard."

"Good God!" They'd got some guts. Four hundred yards away three Mustangs were banking in my direction trying to get on my tail. Three against twenty. Well, good luck to them!

"Heilmann to *Staffel* 9. Go on flying and pay no attention. They think we haven't spotted them. They're trying to get on our tails and then to make a getaway in the clouds."

Thick, black smoke was coming from the exhausts of the Mustangs. They had the greatest difficulty in keeping up with us.

"Get ready. Now's the time. Patt, report, please."

"From Ostro. Victor."

"Patt. Lead your staffel off to the left. All the others follow me in a right-hand turn. A chandelle followed by a tight turn. They must all three think..."

A glance over my shoulder. Yes, now was the time.

"OK, everyone. Wade in on the three Mustangs."

"Victor, Victor, Victor..." came one after the other over the intercom.

I began to count. One, two...

"Hello, boys. If you want to you can count up to fifty."

I looked round with a start. Whose voice was that? I turned my head quickly to the other side and my heart nearly stood still. A host of black dots grew larger against a bank of clouds. Machine after machine dived out of this enormous tower of clouds... oval wings, circles of red, white and blue – Spitfires.

So the Mustangs had called for help. They had flown peacefully behind the Focke formation and had given our course and altitude over their RT. Hence the cynical voice over the intercom. The present frequency of the "*Grünherz*" must be known to them and someone had tuned in on it, in order to jeer at us.

Nice work, Yank, you saved our lives, for a fraction of a second later the "*Grünherz*" would have attacked you and then have had the vastly superior Spitfires on our tails.

I summed up the position in a flash.

The clouds ahead were too far away. We must make a getaway.

We must dive... but through that thick carpet of cloud over there?

"Heilmann calling. To port. Wing tip to wing tip and away to the north."

Before the Spitfires could get into an attacking position – I now estimated them at about fifty – the twenty Fockes with vapour trails streaming behind them, after a series of the tightest possible climbing turns, dived at 350 miles an hour on their pursuers.

Ducking in our cockpits so that we could aim better we began to fire.

Like maniacs Fockes and Spitfires pumped lead into each other's noses. In a flash the exchange of fire was over. The antagonists caught a glimpse of each other as they passed each other at a speed of more that 600 miles an hour.

"Hold on, boys. They'll make things hot for us now. Stick it out."

"OK, Chief. The whole of the Allied Poultry Farmer's Association seems to be fluttering round us today." That was Patt's wisecracking voice, but it did me good to hear it at such critical moments. It was the best medicine for numbing fear and for calming nerves that were stretched to breaking point...

A broad massive bank of clouds sped towards us. Through it...

No easy matter at 400 to 500 miles an hour to dive through this gloomy, milky veil when the aircraft were flying so close together.

The last wisps of cloud and we were through... Barely 3,000 feet below lay the earth. Like shadows of giant sailing ships the clouds cast their silhouettes over the land.

"Ease up a bit. We can't keep up with you."

"Who's calling?"

"Knebe. I've still got three of them with me."

"It's crazy, Kurt. By the time we've slowed to let you catch up we shall be a long way past base. That's Hesepe down there."

What was going on?

Away on the horizon aircraft were circling. Two Me 109s, trailing black smoke, sped towards me. The flak had put up a barrage, then suddenly its fiery fingers turned away to the left and vanished suddenly like a ghost.

Of course. Another dog-fight was in progress. Me 109s and Mustangs. Our poor old soap-boxes would never get away with it.

"Heilmann calling. Stick to me, boys. We must help those poor bastards down there."

Our Fockes burst like a thunderstorm into the fray. There were still a good dozen of us. Fire!

Steep climbing turns, a half-roll and then into the attack again...

Pity, we seemed to have lost our speed. A second attack...

There were a good thirty Mustangs over Hesepe airfield. The flak burst from time to time among them when the moment was favourable. The Mustang pilots must have had a shock, for unfortunately the Tommies or the Yanks only seldom had the unpleasant experience of German fighters cruising round at their massacres.

Six or seven Me 109s lay burning round the airfield. The remaining five profited by the surprise attack of the Fockes and took to their heels, flying low in a westerly direction.

"That wasn't very polite of you," I muttered, pressing the button of my intercom. in the hope that they would hear me, "leaving us up here in the lurch. It wouldn't have been a bad thing to pull your weight." There was no reply.

I had a fleeing Mustang in my sights. It let itself be shot down like a lame duck. Then I gained altitude and was once more above the battle. Their formation badly broken, the enemy were making a last despairing eflfort. Skilful aerobatics left vapour trails near the ground – the inevitable sign that the last ounce of power was being demanded of their machines and that they were throwing them like lunatics about the sky, either to get out of their enemy's sights, or to escape the deadly flak from below. Between Hesepe and Achmer, up to 3,000 feet, the sky was a madhouse. The fighters whirled and twisted in the storm like gigantic swarms of hornets. The fiery tracers glowed harshly in red and yellow arcs, and the fireballs of machines exploding in the air cast their flaming red shadows against the clouds that sailed by above.

The pilots did not appreciate the picture as, dripping with sweat and with frequent black-outs, their hands trembled on the control columns during this fight for life.

There was no need for me to give my men any orders. By now they knew all the snags to be met with in a dog-fight, and time and time again they managed to pull their heads out of the noose.

The circus of death gradually moved northwards. Thanks to the decisive power of their superchargers, the Fockes, which were inferior in numbers, gained superiority over the Mustangs.

"From Heilmann. I must call you offnow. This is the right moment."

Suddenly from above a Mustang dived straight into my sights. A burst of fire. Missed... Never mind... Haven't got time to chase after that little fellow.

"Everyone follow me. Course due north."

With a final, graceful half-roll the Fockes broke off the action. Naturally all of them did not get away unscathed. This was always a terribly anxious moment. Would you get away with it or would you find someone on your tail? The last ones were invariably the victims of fate.

Stop-gaps always die... Today you, tomorrow perhaps me.

* * *

Kurt Knebe had crashed.

Both he and Müller-Berber had been brought down over Osnabrück.

Heini Prager was livid. Kurt was his best friend.

"I can't understand how such a thing could happen."

"For Christ's sake, don't look at me like that as though it were my fault," I said.

"Well, Heilmann, I heard him telling you over the intercom. that he couldn't keep up with you."

"Snap out of it, Heini. You know as well as I do that in a decent stalling turn with the subsequent dive you always leave a rat's tail behind you. That's all part and parcel of air tactics. Anyone who stalls too late and is the last to break off can't catch up with the leaders for at least ten miles."

"I'm sorry, Heilmann. I didn't really mean it. I'm so upset about Kurt. One of the last of the invasion-front boys as you know full well. The whole day he'd been nearly passing out with fright and the only thing I can blame on you is that you shouldn't have let him fly this evening. It was his fourth trip today, you know."

"Prager, remember we're officers, and, as long as the men fly four times a day, we have to do the same thing, at least that's how it ought to be.

Moreover I can't really believe that he was in the Hesepe dog-fight. There were only a dozen of us."

"But he was. It's always better in a crowd. So he and Muller-Berber streaked past and two... Oh, I don't know how many Mustangs must have spotted them, chased them and caught them up on the fifteen-mile stretch to Quakenbrück. I bet they didn't go down without putting up a bloody good fight. It was probably an eye for an eye."

In the meantime I had taken off my flying suit. It was soaked with sweat. I felt in my pockets for a packet of cigarettes. One of the mechanics handed me one.

"Thanks, Michel. How are things apart from that?"

"The 'crates' are just coming in now. Anyhow, the fight must be over, for they can't have any juice left."

"So we all have to be on ops now at the same time," grumbled Prager, banging his cane angrily against his fur-lined flying boots.

"Heini," I warned.

"Oh well, I'm merely looking into the future. In favourable moments – but you have to use rose-coloured glasses to see them – I can see myself grounded and becoming a stationmaster. I'm too much of a bastard to become an angel, otherwise old Prager would now have changed his uniform for wings and a white shift to keep his arse warm..."

In flying circles this was a favourite quip, the stationmaster. On one occasion a pilot home from war who had lost his nerve and suffered from heart or some other form of jitters had taken a job as a stationmaster. Bent double with rheumatism, he would make an imaginary split-arse turn, with his right hand clutching an imaginary joystick, and at the same time imitate the sound of a Spitfire's guns. His head would whip round at the slightest sound, thinking that he'd got someone on his tail.

A cynical form of mockery in the general mood of catastrophe...

Many a pilot would have been happy to have completed his service as a stationmaster, but, crippled and shot up, he was forced to take a barrel-organ and save himself from starvation by begging alms from women and children.

Chapter Nineteen

THE enemy had flung a third bridgehead over the Rhine between Wesel and Rees. Soon the Rhine was no longer a German river, no longer a German frontier but rather a natural obstacle for the enemy. Destruction threatened from the east and a dark shadow lay over Germany forcing a desperate, crazy stream of fugitives almost dead with fright before it. In a short time the tide was lapping against Berlin.

Only an imbecile would not now think of asking for an armistice.

But the man in Berlin, in his bitter disappointment – almost on the border of insanity – held fast to his principles and found no other solution than to drag down a whole people – a great, magnificent, cultured nation – into misery with him.

The miracles had not occurred but the propaganda department kept churning their lying reports into the ears of the people.

Tapper, the Commissar Officer, had ordered the *Kreisleiter* from Kloppenburg to address the *Gruppe* on the defence of the Reich.

I had a conversation with the representative of the Party. He was not a bad fellow and in his own opinion – although he did not voice it – this fanatical continuation of the struggle was absolutely pointless.

I made it quite clear to him that my men would remain true to their oath as long as I, as their commander, continued to give them orders.

"Moreover," I added, "go per cent of them come from East Prussia, or rather they had their homes there. There is no need for me to say any more to you. You can now address my men and it's up to you to find the right note for your speech."

Tapper led the men eagerly to the big messroom where the staffels were assembled.

I had excused myself and my staffel leaders on the plea that there were important briefings to be held for the next day's ops.

A few days later appeared the famous *Oberstleutnant* von Kornatski, a rather large man of about forty from whose eyes energy streamed like flashes of lightning.

He was the leader of the recently formed "suicide *Staffeln*". He was now on a trip trying to recruit pilots.

He addressed the men and kept them spellbound with his fanatical words.

The suicide fighters were to be rearmed. Fewer weapons in exchange for heavier armour-plating. The *Oberstleutnant* had tried them out with his best pilots. He had already developed his own tactics for a ramming attack on a four-engined bomber: attack from below and to the side; attack from behind from a greater height or, even better, from head-on and above. Any "crate" that was not set on fire was to be rammed. It was good enough merely to cut offits tail unit... "But if the worst comes to the worst I myself am perfectly prepared to crash straight into the bomber."

A deathly silence fell upon the pilots when the *Oberstleutnant* finally divulged his reason for coming and let the cat out of the bag. "We must do now what the Japanese did with their *Kamikaze* pilots. I have already had plenty of applications to join my corps. All of us are men who have nothing more to lose, no parents, no wives and no children. Most of us no longer have a home, but in our hearts still burns the resolution to follow the Führer into death.

"Think how many thousands of innocent people, day after day and night after night, fall victim to these murderous fourengined monsters. What is my wretched ruined life if in exchange for it I can save the lives of thousands?"

Then he began to discuss the details.

The pilots who had long since been accustomed to stare death in the eye every day felt the goose flesh rise on their bodies. A strange officer, this *Oberstleutnant* von Kornatski. One could not help believing every word he uttered.

A hero in the truest sense of the word, over whom fame and glory seemed to hang like a halo – a fanatic.

The *Oberstleutnant* kept his word.

Fourteen days, later with a handful of the bravest youngsters, he waded into the bomber formations loaded with explosives and plunged to his death.

* * *

Generalmajor Galland, *Oberst* Trautloft and his whole staff had fallen into disgrace. Some maintained that he was in a concentration camp, while others insisted that he was again flying a *Jagdeschwader* in the south-east.

The great bargain sale had begun.

Within a week it would be Easter.

Ostara, the youthful goddess of re-awakening life and fertility, now appeared as the herald of death.

The left bank of the Rhine was occupied by the enemy. The Russian advance, destroying all before it, burning and raping, swept on towards

Berlin.

In my safe for some days had lain a photostat copy of a map stolen from the American headquarters. It had been printed by the American Operational Department in the Pentagon at Washington. After its theft it was enlarged to six times its size and distributed to the Luftwaffe.

The map showed the splitting up of Germany into zones as was actually done after her collapse. This refuted the obstinate rumours of parole, that diplomatic negotiations were under way, that the Western Powers would only put up a *pro forma* resistance (so our soldiers were to die daily merely *pro forma*!) and that as they advanced they would absorb the remaining German troops who would fight with the Americans against the Russians.

Every soldier knew that since such a map existed Eisenhower had to act and would never allow Montgomery a free hand to be the first in Berlin. The targets for attack had already been worked out – the oil in the Near East, Panslavism with its ageold threat to the Dardanelles and the Near East. Anyone who knew about these things could not for one moment believe in this parole. How long would it be before the Russians and the Americans were at each other's throats? Had bargaining taken place somewhat earlier perhaps such an alliance might have been reached, but now, one moment before the clock struck twelve...

Now Germany was empty-handed and had nothing more to offer or to hope for than an armistice.

* * *

On the 24th March Varrelbusch was heavily attacked by four-engined bombers. The runway survived the raid quite well. The pilots got away with the Fockes and the most important ground personnel to Bissel, a better field some miles to the north. The thick pine forest on the sloping side of the emergency airfield protected the aircraft under its green wing.

Now only free-for-all missions were flown. A few occasional raids were made on the Sauerland and the other attacks were directed on the Remagen bridgehead. Once again our orders were to fly to the Dutch frontier.

Remagen

This mighty 325-yard-long bridge on stone piles with its broad steel span was a heavy item for the pilots to digest. Like a wild cat preparing to spring, the centre span over the soyard-wide river mouth ran on both sides with between eighty and ninety yards of the girders and a network of cables.

A murderous ground defence, such as the pilots had not experienced since the mouth of the Orne, protected this target which was so vital to the enemy. In desperation the High Command, after an audacious underwater attempt to blow up the bridge, ordered a fighter *Staffel* carrying explosive to dive on the bridge.

Only with great eloquence did they succeed in getting this attack postponed until a statement by a high-ranking Pioneer officer could prove that it was futile sending twenty pilots to their death as they could only achieve superficial damage with their small amount of explosive. Moreover it would not be out of action for any length of time, because within five days at the latest the enemy could have built a temporary bridge on the piles.

From now onwards the pilots checked their aircraft very carefully before they took off.

* * *

Now the ground defences were using rockets against the bombers. Only a few of the guns were equipped with them, for this weapon was still in the experimental stage. Wherever it was introduced it had an unqualified success. Two or three of the bombers were quickly brought down.

And next the fighter *Staffeln* were to attack them with similar rockets. They were simply called MR 4's.

The accompanying fireworks of these rockets showed that they were still in a very primitive stage but the High Command could not wait until the steering apparatus had been thoroughly overhauled.

In principle the weapon was quite simple. The 20-in. rockets had two tits on their noses like eyes. These were directional antennae. They were guided to the enemy aircraft by engine noise and radar, and the rockets could be fired at the enemy formations from a safe distance out of range. Only, as has already been mentioned, they were far from being perfect.

The steering apparatus was inefficient.

Thus the fighter formations still had to wade in at the enemy as before, firing their rockets at a maximum range of 300 yards.

* * *

The four-engined bombers had already been airborne for over an hour. The bulk of the stream was now over Haltern. The ground stations thought that the target must be Hanover.

Twenty-five Fockes took off. Eight of the new rockets hung under each wing. The pilots did not feel too happy as guinea-pigs.

At 21,000 feet they made for the enemy formations. The "*Grünherz*" flew in two waves of ten aircraft each led by Dortenmann and Pidder Cromm. With the remaining five machines, I took up my position 1,500 feet above them. I wanted to watch this attack before I ordered the last forty rockets to be fired.

The sky was blue and cloudless, no funk-holes in friendly cloud-banks.

It's of no importance. We're quite high enough. Dive on them and then make a rapid get-away, thought the pilots.

We had spotted the bomber stream from a long way off – a host of silver dots forming an endless fish tail.

Slowly the outlines grew clearer and we recognised the high tail units of the Boeings, a characteristic of these flying fortresses. (This was the bitter irony of war: the accredited designer of the Boeing was apparently a German emigrant engineer.)

The Fockes circled up in the sun. The enemy must not be allowed to spot them too soon. A fighter umbrella of about 100 Spitfires accompanied the stream.

We must wait a bit, I thought. A formation of them will soon be coming without these pretty little Spitfires.

The first waves passed in loose, ragged formation and streaked below the watching German fighters. 3,000 feet below the Mustangs weaved like excitable sheep-dogs round the formation.

Then came a wave of about 300 Boeings without fighter cover.

"Heilmann calling. You take those, Dortenmann. Pidder, you wait a bit."

"Victor." Dortenmann calmly took up his attacking position, too calmly, for in actual fact it was lunacy to attack a stream of four-engined bombers with only ten Fockes.

"Do your stuff, boys!" called Dortenmann. Then they put their noses down and the first wave dived on the enemy. With an advantage in height of 5,000 feet the Fockes attacked ahead from port. With the sun behind them they were not spotted immediately. Only when they fired their rockets did they meet with any reply.

I shan't bother to look any more, I thought as I saw the fiery barrage of bright tracers. Only one in every four bullets was a tracer, to assist us in correcting our aim. The other three – percussion, armour-piercing and incendiary – flew invisible through the air.

Now thin, red trails of fire like comets sped towards the bombers. Those of us who were not in the action held our breath.

Blinded by a harsh glare which burst ahead of the enemy formation, we closed our eyes. A pity... too short.

Dortenmann had pooped off too soon.

"Heilmann to Cromm. Get in closer. Don't fire until you get to 200 yards."

"Victor."

The next barrage of fire was between and in the middle of the bombers.

"Fine work, Pidder. Right on the snout. Cromm and Dortenmann! Scram for home. I'll follow you."

I broke off into a dive followed by the last four Fockes.

The Boeings had split up. There must have been heavy losses among them, for a hail of flying debris spun down among a few parachutes towards the earth.

I wanted to avoid being met by a hail of fire, for five of us would find it unpleasant to have the entire fire directed at us, so I had to dive very steeply in order to get to grips with the remaining Boeings of the last wave.

400... 300... 200... press the button and run for your life.

The sinister red trails of bullets streaked like arrows from our wings. Just below us there was a huge explosion. As if grabbed by ghostly hands and squeezed like a lemon, a dozen Boeings were blown to pieces and fell like a rain of fire to the earth.

Mustangs, Thunderbolts and Spitfires plunged on us from all sides. They were, however, too late. The German fighters had vanished like ghosts.

Another hole had been split in the bomber stream and a dozen parachutes now swayed 3,000 feet below us.

The "*Grünherz*" landed without a casualty and embraced each other in their excitement. Marvellous. No one had expected that. We had destroyed at least forty and probably fifty bombers. This new rocket was just the answer.

But why hadn't it appeared sooner?

The days went by and we waited longingly for more rockets, but we never caught another glimpse of an MR 4.

Naturally it had only been an experiment!

Chapter Twenty

PURSUED by death...

Without compassion and without pity...

Ruthlessly to the bitter end...

Bremen was in British hands. English and Canadian tanks, accompanied by long columns of motorised infantry, pushed forward northwards over the Dummer See and Vechta until they had rounded the lake. The Western Front had now reached the Ems. To the south the Tommies were advancing on a broad front over the Mitteland Canal.

My ground crews were constantly being posted. All my staff officers, even the Adjutant, had left.

Dust-stained, desperate, weeping German girls who had worked with the forces begged every evening to be taken on at Hesepe. They no longer knew to whom they should turn and, as a last resort, they wanted to be with the staffels which had been there just before Christmas.

The "*Blitzmadel*" were like lost souls in the general collapse. The populace more often than not showed them the door. Terrified peasant women chased the fugitives pitilessly out of their houses... In this uncharitableness was a mixture of pious prudery because they looked upon these girls as depraved soldiers' tarts, and fear of being found sheltering the military when the liberator finally marched in. Often they refused these girls the dirtiest corner of their cattle stalls. Their appearance was as unwelcome as a mirror after an attack of smallpox; these people were quite unaware that they should accept things in a spirit of humanity. Cowardice was the order of the day and the Devil was celebrating carnival in Germany. The people of Münster and the Ems were waiting for the British.

The end approached with seven-league boots...

SS troops, who had been fighting bitterly on the right wing ever since the invasion, started to put up a desperate resistance in Holland and had now been pushed back to the marshlands in the West.

A fanatical bitterness lay in this tough fighting. The hard ruthless faces of the officers and the last SS men were merciless with anyone whom they considered to be a coward. A chain of hanged men, with "For Cowardice" signs on their chests, was to be seen along all the retreat roads.

The SS had shown the greatest bravery ever since the first days of the war. In 1939 in front of Modlin in Poland these troops had fought like tigers.

In the terrible winter campaign of 1941-42 at Rjew and Staritza in front of Moscow it was the SS division *Das Reich* which had fought a rearguard with terrible losses covering the retreat of the Ninth Army.

At the hot spots of the invasion front were to be found SS soldiers, near St Lô and at Caen. Sometimes they fought to the last man.

But this record was not entirely spotless. Much blood was shed in vain.

I had been given orders as a last resort to join up with these SS troops.

The High Command had completely lost track of the front.

Now from time to time the "*Grünherz*" flew reconnaissance flights. Each day a red line was marked on the map showing the enemy's advance.

Gefreiter Knell, who had lain with burns for an eternity in hospital, returned to the staffel and was killed on one of these reconnaissance flights. Patt and I were the last two pilots left of the eighty men who had been with the "*Grünherz*" at the time of the invasion.

Pidder Cromm had been involved in a tough dog-fight with Spitfires and was missing. Hans Dortenmann had been transferred to II./JG 26; he took over the command after the death of its *Kommandeur*, *Hauptmann* Worner.

Only about a dozen pilots who had been roped in since Christmas had survived the past three months. More than two hundred had been killed.

I set my jaws and prepared to carry out my last attacks. The weather was more favourable for fighters than it had ever been. The sky was constantly overcast. The spring showers had come and there was rainy weather over the whole continent. April weather...

There was a chance for the skilful pilot now, for the oppressive enemy superiority was not so obvious. If the dogfight grew too tough, one merely disappeared into the clouds.

The "*Grünherz*" made low-level attacks in quick succession.

The advance in the east was towards the Dummer See and Vechta. There was little chance of by-passing this marshy region. Once more we flew together in staffels, and the free-for-all chase was no longer the order of the day.

While Prager returned with six machines and circled over the airfield I took off with two flights. At 600 feet in the clouds the eight Fockes turned southwards, circled over the Mitteland Canal and flew under constant flak as far as Huntekreuzung. Then a change of course to the north and we were above the large, round, staring eye of the Dummer See.

We might be flying round a room, I thought, comparing these short flights with the hour-long trips to the battlefields in the Ardennes. The mouse-trap is about to close and we shall soon be caught in it.

Now we were flying over the main road to Vechta.

Wide sweeps from west to north. We could see a long convoy below. Without fighter cover and uncamouflaged, lorry after lorry... Their flat tin hats pushed back on their heads or hanging on their shoulders, the Tommies stood around smoking cigarettes, presumably taking a halt.

How could they be so damned silly? I was almost sorry for them in their ignorance.

"Perhaps they take us for Mustangs," said *Feldwebel* Pinz from Karlsruhe.

"Could be. I think we'll have a go at them. Hold on a minute."

Eight Fockes sped over the column of trucks. Automatically we carried out our grim task and "wiped the Tommy's eye" as we used to say. The British leaped like madmen into the ditches. There was a trail of burning wagons in the middle of the road.

About turn, and now an attack from the rear because the previous one had been so successful.

Grim rage was the mood over the intercom. You won't get to Bremen as easily as that, my lads!

It'll do you good to get the wind up before you can shout victory.

A fresh attack...

Now the defence guns had woken up, but by this time the whole column was a pile of smoking, burning trucks. Those at least would never reach Bremen.

Three men were firing from behind an armoured screen with a rapid-firing machine-gun. I got it in my sights. Now it was in the cross-wires. Fire!

The gun was out of action. Two of the Tommies had been killed and the third toppled slowly off the truck.

In my excitement I almost hit the ground. My wings grazed one of the trees. Hold hard, I thought to myself. They'll present you with a pretty bill if you have to force-land here.

My Focke bucked and the speed dropped off. I had to put on full right rudder to correct the swing. My comrades had noticed the accident and closed in one on each side of me. Slowly we slipped away and covered the last few miles to Varrelbusch. Soon we could see the big red cross on the roof of the Kloppenburg casualty station.

Shall I let down my wheels or not, I thought?

Better not, I decided. Something might have got jammed or bent when I hit that tree and then they won't lower properly or will break off when I touch down and that would be even worse.

Then I tried the undercarriage buttons.

A quick glance. Port lamp green, then the starboard lamp... green.

Everything OK. Keep her steady. A bit more gas. Down we go.

The Focke bounced like a ball, but I soon got her under control. A few moments later Yellow 6 was taxying along the bomb-damaged perimeter track.

"Poor old Yellow 6," I said to myself as I looked at my Focke at the edge of the airfield. The entire radiator had been torn off, branches and foliage hung in the spinner. I had splintered the prop. It was a miracle that the machine wasn't a write-off. The starboard wing, as far along as the first gun, looked like a compressed accordion.

Well, goodbye, old thing. The Tommies seem to have shot you up a bit.

Lighting a cigarette, I turned round slowly and ambled across the airfield to headquarters. In these days we always had to return on foot. All the trucks had been requisitioned and had been taken by the retreating front-line troops.

In any case what could I do now with my Citroën?

It was better to take the few remaining steps back to the cage on foot. It was good training, for soon I might be pacing up and down behind barbed wire.

⋆ ⋆ ⋆

"What now, sir?"

The *Oberfeldwebel* looked expectantly at me. The whole day we had been burning everything that we would not be using in a week's time – everything that would be of any use to the enemy. Log-books, technical manuals, orders, secret orders, together with the carefully kept top-secret orders, in the fire. Tables, stools, spare parts, parachutes, flying suits, petrol containers, even petrol, anything that came to hand. The Tommies were not far from the airfield and enemy tanks were firing their shells regularly into the nearby fields.

"Round the men up, Michel... and the women are to come too."

"Very good, sir."

I gave my last briefings as *Gruppen Kommandeur*.

The girls were demobilised. They were to wait in their huts until the Allies came in. There was plenty to eat and it was pointless to run away.

"And take care of Tapper and see that he gets his bread and water."

Hauptmann Tapper had been under lock and key for a week. I had found reports on his desk of the pilots' courage or cowardice. I fell into a towering rage when I read the notebooks of this man who had no conception of flying and had probably only been promoted to *Hauptmann* on account of his rank in the Party.

And this loud-mouthed braggart had dared to pass judgment on my pilots, not to mention my officers.

I had waited for the spy with cocked revolver and I had very nearly pressed the trigger in spite of the quaking hands held on high and the terrified chalk-white face. Tapper had understood that his hour had come.

"There are enough poor devils hanging from the trees along your retreat road, you filthy bastard, and I think you've chased enough pilots to their death, eh?"

And then I jabbed my revolver butt into the man's shoulderblades and pushed him through the ranks of grinning airmen to the cellar under the kitchen which served as a cell. A kick in the fellow's backside and he was under lock and key.

Perhaps it would have been best had I shot the swine, I thought. Heini Prager had obviously read my thoughts, for he said loudly so that everyone could hear, "If the Tommies set him free he'll pretend he's a victim and he'll be on the climb again. You know, Willi, in the past few days we should have done better to be in jug. It couldn't be a better recommendation."

The airmen laughed and a few timid girlish laughs could be heard.

Then I dismissed both men and women. I took the NCOs aside. In a few words I made it clear to them that the pilots would fly to Hunstede by Hanover and that the remaining ground personnel could now join the army.

"So for the first time in this war you'll have a gun in your hands. I'm fed up with this eternal retreating. It gets on my nerves and makes me vomit. We were never cowards and every order was carried out as far as we could possibly do so. Hundreds of our dead comrades have proved it with their blood, and their graves bear testimony to it from Kloppenburg to the Normandy coast.

"Now the end is near.

"I'm not retreating any more.

"Make that clear to the reliable men. I can't say it to them. You know that wonderful order that each *gauleiter* has to carry out when the end comes; he can shoot down his cowardly superiors like whimpering curs. There only needs to be one addle-headed fanatic around and I have no intention of getting in the way of one of those ruddy Nazis when he runs amok."

I gave the *Oberfeldwebel* a free hand to find a hide-out on the Galgen moor for a few days with plenty of provisions. I then told the reliable East Prussians that on being given a certain pass word the last men should make their way to the next unit and then disappear into the moor.

They must choose this way out, so that their lives would have some meaning after the collapse. Their women and children were still waiting in the utmost distress to learn the unknown fate of their men and their fathers.

For the last time the engines were rewed up.

While various installations and barracks were blown sky high and the remaining ground staff destroyed the aircraft, machinery and armaments, the pilots took off.

After giving the matter considerable thought I had allowed the pilots to fly off individually or in two's, as they preferred. I could not give the last fourteen pilots an order which I myself would no longer obey. On the other hand, I did not dare to give the order – I could only hint at it – that they should risk a forced landing on the Galgen moor. Each mission of a fighter pilot in its uncertainty, either from weather or contact with the enemy, was a challenge to fate. In this hopeless position there was only one thing to be done: to free the men from my orders and let everyone do what was best for himself.

Who wants to fly to Hanover-Hustede? OK....

Who wants to fly north, perhaps to Oldenburg, which is still in our hands, or to an emergency landing field? OK....

Who in his rnost secret thoughts plans to fly his Focke to his home town, to wives, women or children? OK....

Now we were all airborne, including Prager, Ostro and myself. With moist eyes we waved a last farewell to the mechanics, then pushed our throttles home.

For us this flight would be the leave-taking we had arranged the previous night. I had intended to fly the two hundred miles to the Rhine and force-land near my home town, but then the friendship that existed between us decided otherwise. Patt and I had fought together in a true spirit of comradeship since the invasion in more than a hundred air battles, and of the other officers, Heini Prager was the only man who had survived the past three months.

A last take-off...

We were already making our twelfth farewell circle to gain height. Like eagles we forced our Fockes higher and higher into the sky. After a jubilant circus act round the thick paunch of a cumulus belt at 6,000 feet, we were now striving to reach our ceiling. For the last time we enjoyed to the utmost the indescribable joy of flying. An endless, velvet-blue heaven arched bright and clear above us. At 12,000 feet we put on our oxygen masks.

The Fockes climbed higher in broad spirals towards the sun.

This was to be the last freedom we would be allowed to enjoy. Never again would our hands be allowed the freedom of their controls. Give the mute instruments of war the bitter tears of farewell.

Taste for one last time this flying existence and enjoy the glitter of the aircrafts' bellies in the sun, sparkling higher and higher in the freedom of the air. Towards the sun. Lords of the sky and of its air and clouds for one last time and then it was over.

Down below a bloody sacrifice was drawing to its close. Here at 30,000 feet we no longer smelt the stench of burning, announcing that our country lay there in rubble and ashes.

Yes, Patt. Where is your irrepressible smile and your cheerful whistling which made your freckled Pomeranian stick-out ears look so jaunty? You are weeping.

Heini Prager, the eternal grumbler. The Tommies will now steal your trophies which you arranged so artistically on the walls of your hut. There is a veil before your eyes, too.

Willi Heilmann. Where are your "*Grünherz*"? You have every cause for weeping. The crosses on your pilots' graves stretch in a long chain from Bremen to Caen.

The altimeter showed 36,000 feet.

The Fockes had become flabby and their engines were now not getting sufficient oxygen to take them higher. The air speed indicator lied because the air was too thin for it to be able to register the true speed.

The machines flagged like tired horses. A short climb, and then a weak side slip.

The blue sky changed to a dark, powerful violet. The sun hung like a yellow disc of copper above us. It was an unreal picture, hallucinating owing to the intoxicating oxygen. Could one really see stars in broad daylight in the dark, velvety firmament?

Our bodies seemed to expand and the skin was taut on our cheeks and bellies like balloon coverings.

We circled for a while like giant primeval birds until our fuel-warning lamps started to flicker.

It was our last flight and it had to be lived to the very last moment. Then we sported and tumbled earthwards in a falling leaf. Below us was an enchanted, magnificently beautiful mosaic landscape. Soon we would realise sadly that the stones of the mosaic had been destroyed and crushed to pieces. The world had cut down a fine tree and made a blasphemy of virtue.

The oxygen taps were turned off, and masks removed. The last air circus began. A dog-fight without an enemy, without fear and without death.

In bold sweeps, crazy stalling turns, elegant loops and breathtaking rolls we frolicked down to the earth. A last farewell glance at this bird's-eye view... Forgotten threats... A few tracers climbed towards us...

But no one lit up their screen, no firing should disturb this farewell – this last flight must be pure flying experience.

Now we skirted the crest of the Teutoburger Wald to the north-west, followed the course of the Ems until we had found what we were looking for.

Tenderly, almost with loving care, the last three pilots of the "*Grünherz*" *Gruppe* brought their trusty birds down to land.

Softly the slender bellies of the Fockes sank into the marshy ground.